Leadership
FOR THE
Greater
Good

A TEXTBOOK FOR LEADERS

Dan R. Ebener and Borna Jalšenjak
Foreword by Marty Linsky

Paulist Press
New York / Mahwah, NJ

Cover design by Joe Gallagher
Book design by Lynn Else

Leadership for the Greater Good has been peer reviewed by the following:
• Dr. Kerry L. Priest, Staley School of Leadership Studies, Kansas State University
• Dr. David J. O'Connell, College of Business, St. Ambrose University

Library of Congress Cataloging-in-Publication Data

Names: Ebener, Dan R., author. | Jalsenjak, Borna, author.
Title: Leadership for the greater good : a textbook for leaders / Dan R. Ebener and Borna Jalsenjak.
Description: New York / Mahwah : Paulist Press, 2021. | Includes index. | Summary: "Most of us use the word *leadership* to describe those in authority. This book will argue that leadership can emerge from anywhere, in any context or any organization. The use of coercive, command and control methods fail to engage others in a leadership process. However, those in authority can choose to lead, and can choose to create the structures and build a culture that encourages leadership"— Provided by publisher.
Identifiers: LCCN 2020023078 (print) | LCCN 2020023079 (ebook) | ISBN 9780809155200 (paperback) | ISBN 9781587689154 (ebook)
Subjects: LCSH: Leadership.
Classification: LCC HD57.7 .E234 2021 (print) | LCC HD57.7 (ebook) | DDC 658.4/092—dc23
LC record available at https://lccn.loc.gov/2020023078
LC ebook record available at https://lccn.loc.gov/2020023079

ISBN 978-0-8091-5520-0 (paperback)
ISBN 978-1-58768-915-4 (e-book)

Published by Paulist Press
997 Macarthur Boulevard
Mahwah, New Jersey 07430
www.paulistpress.com

Printed and bound in the
United States of America

To Augustin and Antonija
(*B. Jalšenjak*)
To De, Josh and Paula, Zach and Nikki
(*D. Ebener*)

CONTENTS

FOREWORD

"May you live in interesting times." It is trite to repeat the Chinese curse, which of course is neither Chinese nor a curse. And it has become a cliché to observe that we are living in a period of constant change and unprecedented future uncertainty. But what makes something trite or clichéd is that there is some truth at its center. And my truth, coming from someone with all the perspective and the baggage of having been born before World War II, is that I have never experienced on either a global or personal level the degree of disruption, the relentless shifting of the sand beneath my feet, the challenge to my no longer self-evident truths that are now part of my life.

Daily disorientation has become my daily reality. I know in my head that much of what has enabled me to survive and thrive so far will not be adequate or even useful going forward. And I have no idea in my head or in my heart how to differentiate between which of my tried and true beliefs and behaviors are essential to hang onto, and which ones to provide a decent burial for and leave behind. Like many other people, organizations, and communities, I lurch from seeking a guru to show me the way to the realization that I am as well-positioned as anyone to create the path forward for myself and others. I am both attracted and repelled by those who think they know all the answers. And I am simultaneously energized and humbled by the opportunity to take responsibility for that work myself.

But an opportunity is what it is. The first time I remember hearing the Chinese saying about interesting times was the reporting of a 1966 speech by Robert Kennedy in Cape Town. Most important for our purposes, Kennedy found the phrase a source of optimism and hope in what was also a chaotic period. After quoting the proverb, here's what he went on to say: "Like it or not we live in interesting times. They are times of danger and uncertainty; but they are also more open to the creative energy of men than any other time in history."

We are in the midst of another moment of instability and concomitant opportunity. Yes, our twentieth-century understanding of leadership does not fit the times we are in. However, that very uncertainty creates possibility, the need for creativity and innovation, for leaving behind those ideas and assumptions that may have served us well but are no longer relevant or useful, and for taking the best of what we know and bringing it forward, setting it in the current context, tweaking, massaging, amending, and, yes, adapting it to the new reality.

That is what Dan Ebener and Borna Jalšenjak have done in the pages that follow. Their book is full of hope, balanced with an awareness of what is needed, and leavened with tools for getting the work done in a way that minimizes the risks and maximizes the chances of making progress. The work of leadership, helping people in your company or your community tackle their most difficult problems, is never easy, in any era. If you want to lead change in your organization or your neighborhood, you can do so whatever your role or your position, believing in the possibilities while mindful about what it will take. Our coauthors set out to use their roles, their platform as teachers, to try to lay out a conceptual understanding of leadership fit for our times, with practical guidance for how to do it. It is a call to act on whatever is keeping you awake at night. You can do this.

Exercising leadership in this time of uncertainty is made more complex because of difficulty of sustaining a place of moderation and nuance in the center. I have always enjoyed having one foot on the boat and one on the dock. Elective politics, my first love along with the Boston Red Sox, has always been a hostile environment for centrism. An election is a competition, an explicit pursuit of authority, a powerful centrifugal force, pulling society apart, emphasizing difference until after the votes are counted. But there always has been the ritualistic postelection peaceful transfer of power, and the great coming together. In today's binary self-righteous world, however, the election never ends, the conflict at the office is never over, the coming together never happens. The winners keep moving the goalposts, and the losers are at risk of being ghosted or canceled (whichever appellation of near-extinction irrelevance my millennial friends would consider most applicable).

And that is a very big problem, whether we are talking about politics (which always surface and mirror broader cultural and community issues), about the great societal challenges such as race and climate change, or about the tough issues you are dealing with at work or, for that matter, in your personal life as well. The hollowing out of the center makes the stakes existential and the risks primal. On the other hand, essential to the stability in the nation or in your workplace is that the losers in the resolution of a particular conflict see a place of dignity and respect for themselves in the picture postcard of the future as portrayed by the winners. I spent some time in Northern Ireland during the turmoil known as the Troubles. It was not until the Republicans could describe a future in which the Loyalists could see themselves comfortably that they could lay down their arms. Similarly, it was Nelson Mandela's courageous and extraordinary sharing of power with Frederik de Klerk that enabled de Klerk's losing side to commit to a peaceful if painful transition and an end to the violent resisting of the inevitable shift to a multiracial structure of authority.

Politics is a stand-in for the norms of surfacing and addressing difficult value-laden issues and conflicts in any society. What does it mean to exercise leadership when each faction sees those with a different perspective as the enemy and its own point of view as right in some fundamental way? How do you exercise leadership in a binary world where compromise is seen as unprincipled and playing with those on the other side is condemned? How does someone help a community preserve what is essential from the past when the conversation is dominated by those who believe there is nothing worth preserving and those who believe that every element of it must be retained or regained? We need a new synthesis to apply what we know about leadership to where we are, a fifth of the way through the twenty-first century.

In my dotage, I am not ambitious enough to try. I am excited that Dan Ebener and Borna Jalšenjak have risen to the challenge in the pages that follow, distinguishing among all the leadership ideas, principles, and tactics that have come before and may have made sense at one point or another, and identifying those which are of the essence and which need to be left behind.

I do want to underscore some thoughts about what we have learned that are honored in this book and seem especially fundamental to preserve.

First, leadership is inextricably tied to loss. Radical empathy, having deep understanding of and paying attention to those who fear or experience loss, is essential to survival and success.

Second, the hard work of leadership, particularly in a world of heightened faction and identity consciousness, is not about bringing undecideds and skeptics along, but bringing your own faction along, for they will undoubtedly be upset at your consorting with the enemy. Leadership requires disappointing your own people at a rate they can absorb.

If you have read this far, you must be interested in saving the world, at least that part of it over which you feel you have some agency. Great. The tumultuous times need you. Your company and your community need you to step up, perhaps more than ever before in our lifetimes. But when things get tough, resist falling into cynicism or floating off into naivete. Hold tightly to both your *relentless optimism* about the possibility of change and your *hard-nosed realism* about what it will take to do so. Don't let the system pressure you into choosing between the two.

You can do this, and you will be much more effective in doing so after absorbing what follows here.

Marty Linsky
New York
February 25, 2020

PREFACE

Why another textbook on leadership? As leadership professors, we have experimented with dozens of textbooks. Generally, they give too much attention to theories that describe a world that no longer exists. Here we will try to move beyond that yesteryear mindset and pay closer attention to the complexities of practicing leadership in a twenty-first-century organization.

We have been teaching leadership together since 2010. We decided to write our own text to engage and inspire the next generation of leaders. Here is what we plan to do:

1. Give priority to the leadership approaches that address today's reality: as we see it, leadership is about adapting to an increasingly complex world.
2. Practice academic integrity, using the word *leadership* only when we are describing the voluntary, interactive activity that we will define as leadership.
3. Search the traditional "leadership" theories for the significance they might still have in the context of today's organizational environment.
4. Present our case for leadership as an activity that enhances "the greater good."
5. Use plain and concise language.

This book was originally intended for use as a textbook for colleges and universities. Upon its completion, we circulated it among friends and colleagues for feedback. What they told us is that we had written a book that was not only a textbook for scholars but a guide for practitioners. Several of our friends in business said they could not wait to order copies of the book for their leadership teams. So, we offer the book as both a primer and a textbook, with the hope that people will not only change their minds about leadership but change the way they lead for the greater good.

Leadership for the greater good means leading for a purpose that goes beyond profit. Profit is a *means* toward an end. It is not the purpose of business. The purpose of business is the advancement of society and the fulfillment of human lives. Leadership is a bold move that inspires people with a sense of purpose. We agree with Robert Greenleaf, who stated that business should exist for people, not the other way around.[1]

Business has changed but business models have not. Leadership has changed but leadership theories have not. Too many books, articles, and blogs on leadership are stuck in a mindset that leadership is providing people with clear directions and supervising them to make sure they comply. To compete in today's global business world requires more than giving directions, providing supervision, and gaining compliance. Organizations that succeed today must *engage* their people.

Joseph Rost, a leadership scholar whose work on defining leadership is the most robust we have found, suggests that traditional theories of leadership fall into these categories: Leadership as Transformation; Leadership as Excellence; Leadership as Charisma; Leadership as a Set of Traits, Skills, or Behaviors; Leadership as the Achievement of Goals; or Leadership as "Do What I Say."[2]

Rost illustrates how each of these approaches is flawed. The language they use assumes that leadership emerges from hierarchical authority. Generally, these theories are about "good management." This does not render them irrelevant, but their value is limited to instances where people are practicing leadership while holding a formal position of authority.

A major theme in this book is that leadership can be practiced *with or without* positional authority.[3] We will explain how and why leading from a position of authority is no easy task, given the temptation to over-rely on the use of formal authority. We believe that leadership without authority can begin when you see something that needs to change and you influence others to join you in a change process—as long as the followers do so of their own volition.[4] We will discuss what those in formal authority can do to encourage the more informal practice of leadership.[5]

We understand that some people may struggle with the concept of leadership without authority. Many organizations appoint plenty of people to positions of authority yet still struggle with the lack of leadership. If those people in authority lean toward a more autocratic style, they will discourage any practice of leadership—with or without authority. We will make the case that a more democratic style can enhance the greater good of business and society.[6] This is what we mean by leadership for the greater good.

In part 1, we will give priority to the newer approaches to leadership and how it can be practiced. We will focus on (1) *adaptive* leadership, which is leading change for which there are no technical solutions;[7] (2) *engagement*, which is intrinsically motivating leaders and followers to address adaptive challenges;[8] and (3) the *ethics* of leading in an increasingly complex world.

In part 2, we will review the dominant traditional theories, most of which address "good management."[9] We will try to salvage what we think is most useful from these theories and apply those lessons to the practice of leadership in today's complex organizations. What we find most relevant from these older theories might be most helpful to those trying to practice leadership while holding a formal position of managerial authority.

In part 3, we will describe and explain what we think are best practices in leadership today. We will explore a set of four skills we think are necessary for leading change with or without a position of authority: (1) *emotional* skills, such as self-awareness, self-control, social awareness, and social skills associated with emotional intelligence;[10] (2) *dialogical* skills, such as asking open questions and listening with an open mind;[11] (3) *conflict* skills, such as finding a more collaborative path to different types of conflict;[12] and (4) *strategic* skills that cocreate a plan and action steps toward mutual purposes or a shared vision.[13]

In our introduction, we will define leadership. Throughout this book, we will abide by that definition. In that way, we will avoid conflating the word *leadership* with other activities such as management. We will use the word *leadership* only when it is consistent with our definition of it. Otherwise, we will place "leadership" in quotation marks.

———————————————————————

Editor's Note: The writing of this book was completed prior to the COVID-19 pandemic.

ACKNOWLEDGMENTS

We owe a great many debts to a great many people who have contributed to this book with their advice, support, and generally putting up with us during the time we were writing it. Here we would like to expressly thank a few of them, knowing full well that we will forget someone, so we would like to use this opportunity to extend our gratitude to them as well and apologize for any unintentional oversight.

Our students gave us valuable input regarding the ideas in this book, but we would like to especially thank the students who were the very first to read the manuscript in its early stages during the summer course at St. Ambrose University in 2019. They are Guilbert Ebune, Carlie Nelson, Kelsey Pence, Caleb Rangel, and Ebony Rivers. Their ideas made it into this final version of the book.

Our colleagues provided us with invaluable dialogue, support, and feedback on various drafts of the manuscript. So, thank you to Randy Richards, Ron Wastyn, Kristijan Krkač, Amy Grotewald, Kevin James, David O'Connell, Jane Rutter, Fr. Francis Odoom, Mary Macumber Schmidt, Linda Frederiksen, Fred Smith, Steve Ambrozi, Danielle Ebaugh, Kelly Dybvig, Terry Poplava, Teresa Keogh, Stacy Speidel-Holke, and Phil Hart. We give our warmest thanks to our reviewers who have graciously dedicated their time and expertise to improve this book.

Our institutions were kind to offer their support in the creation of this book, so we would like to thank St. Ambrose University, Luxembourg School of Business, and Zagreb School of Economics and Management.

We would also like to thank Dr. Kerry L. Priest, Staley School of Leadership Studies, Kansas State University; and Dr. David J. O'Connell, College of Business, St. Ambrose University, for their time and talent as peer reviewers for this book.

Finally, thank you to Cheri Boline for her help with the charts in this book, and thanks to Donna Crilly and to Paulist Press for making this book a reality.

INTRODUCTION
LEADERSHIP AND MANAGEMENT

Organizations need leadership because they need change. They need internal change that adapts to the constant and rapid changes of the outside world. Challenges born in the outside world demand change inside their organizations. This change requires leadership. Leaders identify and tackle the challenges that the outside world presents. All leadership involves change, even if not all change involves leadership.

Generally, the study of leadership is the art and science of change. It is an art that requires improvising, adjusting, and adapting to a world where the challenges can be relentless and where the playbook cannot cover all the myriad situations that leadership entails. It is a science because there is a wealth of scholarly literature—drawing from sociology, psychology, philosophy, and political science—written about virtually every aspect of leadership.

As the pace, complexity, and endurance of change in the world continues to grow, the demand for leadership also grows. Without leadership, our organizations lose ground to the competition. They are subjected to the adage, "If you're not growing, you're dying."

LEADING WITH OR WITHOUT A POSITION OF AUTHORITY

Theoretically, most people agree that leadership can be exercised with or without authority. However, their actions speak otherwise. In practice, most assume that only those with authority can lead. They figure that only those with titles and positions are real leaders.

Likewise, most "leadership" textbooks begin with a statement that "leadership" can be practiced with or without authority. However, the rest of their text speaks otherwise. They focus uncritically on theories that use the word *leader* as synonymous with supervisor, manager, and others in authority. This is a source of frustration and confusion for our students.

We will demonstrate here that *anyone* can lead change—with *or* without positional authority. Having formal authority has some obvious advantages with its access to resources and decision-making. Leading without formal authority also has advantages, such as being unencumbered by managerial responsibilities.

People without authority are more likely to step up and lead when and if those in authority step back and create the space for others to lead. One of the primary functions of authority is to nurture the culture, to form the structures, and to craft the strategies that can allow and encourage those without authority to step up and lead.

Those with positional authority can also choose to lead and not rely solely on their positional power. They can lead without using their formal authority. Leading without authority can achieve more buy-in, motivate more intrinsically, and reach longer-lasting results.

When the culture of an organization is more authoritarian, it can be countercultural to practice some of the leadership activities we present in this text. And even when the culture is less authoritarian, it can be difficult for those with authority *not* to be heavy-handed because it is faster and easier to dictate than to delegate. It is faster and easier to monologue than to dialogue. It is faster and easier to impose your will than to discern the will of your team.

To get leadership results, such as engagement, those in authority must make the conscious choice to consult and involve more people in decision-making. If you want to get buy-in, you must allow others to weigh in. When people are not allowed to participate in decisions that affect their lives, they feel more distant and less motivated.

The key to leading *with* positional authority—which can be done—is to resist the temptation to rely solely on that authority. Paradoxically, if you want to lead when you have formal authority, you need to influence as if you do not have that authority. When you are relying on your positional authority, in that moment, with that activity, you are *not* leading.

If you feel a sense of urgency about changing something, it is your choice whether you step up to lead or not. No one can appoint you as a leader. They can encourage or discourage your leadership. Ultimately, it is your individual choice to lead or not. When you grow concerned about changing something, and you begin to influence others to join you in a change effort, and they join you voluntarily, you are leading—whether you have authority or not.

With a position of authority, sometimes you are expected to lead *and* to manage. As John Kotter teaches, leaders deal with change and managers deal with complexity.[1] Those with authority must deal with both change and complexity. Given the daily grind and urgent demands of management, it is easy to succumb to the *tyranny of the urgent* and become more inclined to manage than to lead. The urgency of the work of management can trump the importance of the work of leadership. The constant demands of management can distract from the activity of leadership.

Nevertheless, management can play a key role in creating (1) the cultural norms that encourage initiative and creativity, (2) the flatter structures that allow for shared leadership, and (3) the bold strategies that support leadership so it can emerge from surprising places. On the other hand, when people feel stifled with micromanagement, or when those in authority discourage initiative, or when they restrain people from taking even prudent risks, the people will be less likely to lead. Hence, an organization that is overmanaged is sure to be underled.

USING THE WORDS *LEAD* OR *LEADER*

The common use of the word *leader* is perplexing. News sources describe government officials as "leaders," even if they are despots and dictators. The people at the top of most businesses are called "leaders," and those at the very top are called "senior leaders." Owners, board members, and top management teams are automatically considered "leaders."

Because we have been studying, teaching, coaching, consulting, and writing about leadership for decades, we have become very judicious about the use of the word *leader*. It should mean more than the best, biggest, fastest, strongest, or the person at the top. The problem is that the word *leader* is in the common vocabulary, and it means something very different there than it will here in this book. We believe that using the word *leader* to include everyone who makes their way to the top is a disservice to the whole idea of leadership. It discourages the practice of leadership.

As our friend and colleague Randy Richards points out, most people assume that "leadership" is about casting a vision and then selling it to others. That is yesterday's notion of leadership—clearly not consistent with the practice of leadership as we will discuss it here.

We believe our organizations, and our world, desperately need leadership for the greater good. The culture, structures, and strategies of modern organizations need to adapt to a world that has changed and is changing. If people see leadership merely as positional, they will wait for leadership instead of practicing it. A major theme in this book is that leadership can emerge from anywhere—not only from seats of formal power.

DISTINGUISHING LEADERSHIP FROM MANAGEMENT

So, what does it mean to be a leader? How can we break through the noise of our language and our culture that confuses leadership with titles, positions, and hierarchy?

When we are asked to conduct leadership retreats, we sometimes begin with an exercise called *concept mapping*. We break into small groups of four or five people and ask them to draw a picture of leadership without using words.

Most people begin by drawing images that project "leadership" as a position of authority. They often place the "leader' at the top or in the center of their pictures. "Leaders" are usually drawn with bright colors, strong muscles, big hearts, huge ears, and loud voices. "Leadership" pictures are characterized with smiley faces, mountain tops, finish lines, rainbows, and sunshine. Those being "led" are smiling, holding hands, and having fun.

Then we ask people to draw a picture of *management*. The managers are also seen as those at the top. But with managers, the drawings usually include hard lines, squares, rectangles, and arrows that depict flow charts and lines of authority. Those being managed look grim. They show fear, sadness, or boredom on their faces. Sometimes, the people being managed are depicted as simple cogs in a wheel. Gone are the bright colors, big hearts, and strong muscles— although the loud voices often remain.

The distinctions between leadership and management become clearer when we post all the pictures on a wall and ask people to look for patterns. We ask *open*, probing questions such as, How does leadership appear in these pictures? Why does management look so grim? How is the relationship in leadership different from that of management? What is the role of change?

This exercise launches critical conversations. Upon further reflection, most people begin to see that leadership is *not* all sunshine and smiley faces, and that it certainly does not have to be depicted as the person who is the biggest, strongest person at the top. They recognize that leadership can be practiced by people at the top, bottom, and throughout an organization.

They also realize that management does *not* have to be so foreboding. They begin to question the mistaken notion that *leadership is good* and *management is bad.*[2] This exercise helps people realize that both leadership and management are essential for organizational success. We conclude the exercise by asking the participants to summarize what they have learned, and we create a chart such as this:

Leadership	Management
(1) *Strategizes* for change	(1) *Structures* the order in a workplace
(2) Involves a *voluntary* and *interactive* relationship	(2) Involves an *authority* relationship
(3) Co-creates a *shared* vision or mutual purposes	(3) Administers *operational* functions such as human resources, finance, and technology

Chart 1: Leadership and Management

Viewed separately, leadership and management are necessary but not sufficient. Viewed together, they offer a full range of functions needed for organizational success: Managers develop structure. Leaders deliver strategy. Managers provide security. Leaders promote change. Management adds structure to organizational life. Leadership adds life to organizational structures.

Management must be authorized by someone in a hierarchical authority. Leadership cannot be authorized by anyone in hierarchical authority. It is authorized by the person who chooses to lead. Management is a position. Leadership is a choice.

OUR DEFINITION

After considering hundreds of definitions, we have gravitated toward the work of two authors, Joseph Rost and Ronald Heifetz, in defining leadership as

"a voluntary, interactive process that intends adaptive change."

The activity of leadership begins when you decide to change things. You invite, influence, or inspire others to join you in a change effort. When others begin to join you—*voluntarily* join you—then you are leading.

Leadership engages others in a mutual influence process. Leaders influence followers and followers influence leaders. Leaders often begin by practicing followership, which becomes preparation for taking a turn at leadership.

Leadership with authority can be hard to distinguish from *good management.* Both require many of the same traits such as wisdom, humility, and courage. They require similar behaviors such as motivating, delegating, and building trust. They require the same skills such as listening, summarizing the ideas of others, and advocating your own viewpoint.

The distinctive factors are the following: (1) leadership is *voluntary,* which means no one is being coerced into the change process; (2) leadership is *interactive,* which means the communication goes in multiple directions, allowing leaders and followers to mutually influence each other; and (3) leadership intends *adaptive* change, which involves real changes in the culture, structure, or strategies of the organization (chapter 1).

The focus of management is order, structure, and control. In management, it is clear who the authority figure is. Managerial positions do not change from day to day, whereas in leadership, the change agent can and should rotate at various stages of the change process. Such rotation becomes more difficult when some members of the team have authority over others.

Leadership gets complicated when the change agent is also a person in a position of formal authority, especially when the "leader" is charismatic or when others report directly to that person. The tendency is to heap unquestioning loyalty on the charismatic person or those in authority. Generally, the higher the authority, the more positive the praise, the less honest the feedback—and the less likely that leadership will be practiced.

Leadership with authority does have certain advantages, with its access to financial assets, human capital, and other resources. However, with more authority comes more temptation to rely too heavily on that authority— because using authority to dictate change can seem easier.

When we conduct leadership trainings, we usually are contracted by the CEO or people at the top, who will often say, "We want our people to lead, not manage." We believe what they are saying is that they want their people (usually their middle managers) to rely on intrinsic motivators that will produce more "above and beyond" behavior from the workers, instead of relying solely on formal authority and extrinsic motivators. Workers respond with more enthusiasm when they are engaged (intrinsically motivated) by leadership.

The CEO of a company, the general of an army, or the best player on a football team is likely to be proclaimed a "leader." Not in this textbook. Here we will use extreme caution when calling someone a "leader" or something "leadership." If leadership is a core value—and it is for us—then how we define it is more than a scholarly exercise. Its definition can change the very practice of the leadership that we think the world so desperately needs.

PART I
LEADERSHIP TODAY

INTRODUCTION

Management was invented by the industrial era. The whole idea of management became necessary when industrial organizations grew so large that owners could no longer hire only family and friends. When businesses grew beyond their ability to manage, the owners hired managers who would hire the workers and supervise them.

As businesses evolved into large corporations, owners were assumed to be "leaders." They were expected to have the vision and tell the middle managers what to do. The middle managers would tell the workers what to do and supervise them to make sure they did what they were told.

If something went wrong, the middle managers were expected to know the solution—or to bring in an expert. The "leaders" made the tough decisions and tried to sell their ideas down the line. It was not important to seek the advice, the perspective, or the feedback of the middle managers—yet alone the workers.

Salary and benefits were enough to motivate workers to get the job done. People were hired for technical skills. A paycheck gained compliance. People did their jobs. Top performers were rewarded with promotions to become bosses. They relied on their technical skills to tell people what to do and to solve technical problems that arose.

That world has changed—and is changing ever more rapidly. The more interconnected the world has become, the more these global changes are affecting everyone in every country, every culture, and every society on the planet. What happens in one corner of the world surely impacts other corners of the world.

Global changes in economic systems, advances in technology, innovations in communications, dependence on global supply chains, geopolitical tensions, migration of large numbers of people, and other developments have shaken the world and changed the way we should think about leadership and management.

As the world becomes more complex, businesses require workers with more creativity to come up with new ideas and the courage to present them to those in authority. If workers are to change, the way leaders lead them must change.

"Leadership" theories of the past lack the dynamism to conceive of these changes. The very constructs of "leadership" need to be reimagined. Some of that new thinking and research is emerging. As DeRue and Ashford put it, "Theorists have begun to conceptualize leadership as a broader, mutual influence process independent of any formal role or hierarchical structure and diffused among the members of any given social system."[1]

DeRue suggests that leadership is a social interaction process where "relationships are influenced but not entirely constrained by formal authority structures."[2] This social interaction or mutual influence process is a "reciprocal" relationship where leaders and followers influence each other to imagine new ways of doing things.[3] Because this interactive process of mutual influence is not determined by positional power or rank, the dominant theories no longer apply. The theories of the past need to be reevaluated with a look toward the future.

Leadership for the greater good is an approach that shifts the emphasis toward (1) inspiring people with a sense of purpose about their work, (2) serving that purpose with the honesty and integrity that builds trust, (3) seeking input and gaining buy-in from workers to attempt adaptive strategies, (4) advancing beyond the simple goal of gaining compliance by learning the art of creating a culture of active engagement, (5) building structures that allow workers to participate in shared leadership and shared decision-making, (6) changing organizational cultures to build more capacity for adaptive leadership, and (7) committing to a purpose that extends beyond profits and toward the common good of society.

In chapter 1, we will describe, explain, and define the *task* of leadership—what needs to change and how to change it. We will make the case that the business world needs *adaptive* change, and therefore adaptive leadership.[4] As Marty Linsky suggests in the foreword to this book, this includes developing a capacity for dealing with the uncertainty that comes from a changed and changing world.

In chapter 2, we will focus on the *relationship* side of leadership. As the business world has become more socially, culturally, and organizationally complex, and as the need for adaptive change grows, leaders need to engage their people by building trust, demonstrating care, valuing their insights, and intrinsically motivating them.

In chapter 3, we will focus on leadership ethics. Businesses find themselves in complex situations today that raise questions of ethics and morality. We believe that looking at the applied ethics of leadership can help reduce the cost of making questionable decisions and expensive mistakes. It will also help us understand the ethics of the leader-follower relationship.

CHAPTER 1

THE TASK OF LEADERSHIP

A POSTINDUSTRIAL UNDERSTANDING

In 1991, Joseph Rost recognized that the world of business was becoming less industrial. He provided a "postindustrial" definition of leadership as "an influence relationship among leaders and followers who intend real changes that reflect their mutual purposes."[1] In this definition, Rost uses these four factors to define leadership: (1) influence relationship, (2) leaders and followers, (3) intend real changes, and (4) mutual purposes.

(1) *The influence relationship* must be noncoercive and multidirectional. That means the interactions between leaders and followers flow in all directions. It also means that leaders and followers can change places. Leadership can emerge from anywhere, but it cannot be simply based on authority or positional power.[2]

(2) *Leaders and followers* are the active participants in the relationship that creates leadership. The followers in the relationship must be active. This means they are participating in the relationship with other followers and a leader. It is possible for people to be leaders in some relationships and followers in others.[3]

(3) *Intend real changes* means leaders and followers work toward substantive and transforming "changes in people's lives, attitudes, behaviors and basic assumptions, as well as in the groups, organizations, societies, and civilizations they are trying to lead."[4] The change must make a real impact on people's lives. "Intends" means that leaders and followers may fail to achieve real change, at least in the short run, yet still be involved in leadership.

(4) *Mutual purposes* are the reasons that leaders and followers come together.[5] Rost distinguishes mutual purposes from the "common goals" used in many definitions of leadership, including those of Peter Northouse[6] and James MacGregor Burns.[7] Generally, a purpose is more qualitative than a goal. While the "goal" might be to increase sales by 10 percent, the purpose might be to change the way sales works with marketing. Management focuses on more quantitative goals, while leadership works on the more qualitative change, the mutual purposes.

ADAPTIVE LEADERSHIP

Ronald Heifetz calls it *adaptive leadership*.[8] This means leading organizations through adaptive challenges, which require an organization to adapt *internally* to changes that are occurring *externally*. Adaptive leadership creates the capacity "to change guided by a purpose that generates progress."[9] It can happen with or without authority.

Adaptive leadership brings people together to solve an adaptive problem and mobilizes them to bring about adaptive change. Exercising adaptive leadership does not depend on a position.[10] Anyone can practice adaptive leadership when they (1) influence others to join them in identifying the adaptive challenge, (2) persuade others to recognize the mutual purpose of addressing that adaptive challenge, and (3) involve others in activities that intend real changes.

Most adaptive leadership emerges from those without authority, which is what makes it so dangerous. Ronald Heifetz and Marty Linsky warn that adaptive leadership appears dangerous because it questions values, beliefs, and habits.[11] Adaptive leadership requires that you challenge the status quo, confront tacit assumptions, and shape the way people think, plan, decide, and work.

As Marty Linsky emphasizes in the foreword to this book, adaptive change involves loss. The change that transforms an organization demands that people sacrifice things they hold dear, such as their ways of thinking, acting, and relating to each other.[12] In return, they are offered nothing more than the possibility of a better future.

Resistance to adaptive change is based on a sense of anger, fear, and sadness about what is being sacrificed. In adaptive change, people are likely to go through the Elisabeth Kübler-Ross stages of grief: (1) denial, (2) anger, (3) bargaining, (4) sadness, and (5) acceptance.[13] Leadership must acknowledge the loss and inspire people to what can be gained by the adaptive change.

Change is at the heart of leadership. If you are not changing something, you are not leading. You might be managing, administering, or fixing something.

However, it is not leadership unless it involves change. Leaders stimulate adaptive change. Unless you are willing to generate some newness, you will get the same results you always got.

Leading change is living on a threshold. Leadership thrives on the doorstep of change. Professor Margaret Wheatley says that leadership dwells in that part of the world where the old is giving way to the new.[14] Leaders see with eyes that listen. They hear with ears that see. They feel with hearts that understand those who are hurting. As Robert F. Kennedy stated, leaders imagine things that might be and ask, *Why not?*[15]

The biological principle of *entropy* applies here. It suggests that every living thing—every plant, every animal, and every person—is in the process of dying. If you think of your organizations as having life and energy, then entropy is a threat. If people are not breathing new and positive energy into their organizations, adapting to the external changes occurring in the world, their organizations will die from entropy.

Change is constant. Ignoring the external change that is outside your control—or resisting the internal change that is inside your control—leaves your organization vulnerable to entropy. As Leon C. Megginson paraphrased Charles Darwin as saying, "It is not the most intellectual of the species that survives; it is not the strongest that survives; but the species that survives is the one that is able best to adapt and adjust to the changing environment in which it finds itself."[16] Organizations that are not adapting are dying.

ADAPTIVE VERSUS TECHNICAL SOLUTIONS

Ronald Heifetz was a medical doctor before he became an organizational expert. He coined the term *adaptive challenge* after reflecting on his medical practice. Patients search for easy solutions to their health problems. They want the doctor to prescribe a pill, conduct a procedure, or do something that makes their medical problems quickly go away. Heifetz found that most patients wanted him to make their problems disappear but were unwilling to change their own daily habits, even when those habits were the cause of their medical condition.[17]

The same can be said for organizations, where people also look for quick answers and easy solutions. According to Heifetz, Grashow, and Linsky, "Adaptive challenges can only be addressed through changes in people's priorities, beliefs, habits, and loyalties."[18] Adaptive change requires a change in hearts and minds. That is why adaptive change can be so challenging.

Adaptive issues require analysis, research, and discussion. They require a change in attitude, behavior, or values. If you are prone to catching a cold, you may need to change your diet, schedule, and routines. If you have a bad back, you may need to change the way you lift, what you carry, and how long you sit. These would be adaptive changes. Most people are interested only in the technical fix, which is an easy answer and a known solution.[19]

Most problems have technical and adaptive aspects. Let's say you have a lower back problem. Pain killers might offer temporary relief. Surgery may solve a technical problem in your lumbar system. But if you are unwilling to do the adaptive work, such as physical therapy afterward, and changing some of your daily habits, your back problems will resurface.

TECHNICAL VS. ADAPTIVE

Let's say you have a flat tire. You repair the tire (a technical fix). Your problem may be solved. However, if you have another flat tire the next day, and the next, you should look for the cause of the flat tires. Maybe you need to remove the roofing nails from your driveway (another technical fix). Maybe you need to change the way you drive (an adaptive challenge).

The adaptive approach looks more systemically at the problem. A technical fix only works when and if the problem is only technical. Adaptive challenges require more than a technical fix. They require a change of hearts, minds, and habits.

IDENTIFYING ADAPTIVE CHALLENGES

Heifetz, Grashow, and Linsky define technical challenges as known solutions, ones that can be implemented with current know-how.[20] Adaptive challenges require new thinking. The table below presents core differences in the two kinds of challenges.[21]

Heifetz describes three types of organizational challenges: Type I challenges are technical in nature. Type II are the most common challenges, with some technical and some adaptive elements. Type III are adaptive challenges that threaten the very life of the organization.[22]

Heifetz also points out that people are conditioned to defer to authority, which helps to explain why organizations usually attempt to fix an adaptive problem with technical know-how.[23] People in authority often are promoted because of their technical expertise. They figure they are being paid to come up

Technical Challenges tend to be...	Adaptive Challenges tend to be...
Easier to identify	Harder to identify
Quick and easy fix	Changes in hearts and minds
Authority or expert can solve	People closest to the problem can solve
Simpler change	Systemic or cultural change
People are more receptive	People are more resistant
Solutions can be implemented by edict	Takes longer to implement

Chart 2: Adaptive vs. Technical Challenges
based on Heifetz, Grashow, and Linsky

with solutions that rely on their technical skills to solve the problems they see. Unlike adaptive solutions, which require that people change, technical fixes are often well-accepted by the people who want a quick and easy solution.

Adaptive challenges are difficult to identify and easy to ignore. Many people do not see past the technical aspects of problems, or if they do, they do not want to deal with the consequences, so they just push it off.[24] They deny adaptive change to avoid the loss associated with adaptive problems. They do not want to give up something that has value.

Adaptive challenges can be more readily identified by people when they know how to ask the right questions. As Michael Marquardt points out, "Questions about strategy, vision, and values should not be treated as technical problems—but as adaptive problems."[25] He says that to deal with adaptive problems, people need a forum for active debate, to drive the organization to find new questions rather than easy answers.

AN ENGINEERING FIRM

Let's say that you have an engineering company that bids on new construction. You respond to requests for proposals by asking your engineers to estimate what it would cost to do the engineering for that project. Let's assume that the construction world now only accepts proposals under a general contractor who works with engineers, carpenters, electricians, plumbers, roofers, and other contractors. Instead of individual proposals that focus only on engineering, now you have to submit one joint proposal.

This external change presents an adaptive challenge that requires an internal change. Engineers known for their technical skills will need to develop collaborative skills of negotiation, or else the company will be unable to obtain new work. This could literally put the organization out of business.

In this example, the environment changed, which required the engineering firm to adapt. In the new environment, the firm needs to find or develop people with negotiation skills. This could be viewed as an opportunity to encourage leadership to emerge from within the ranks of the engineers who could be negotiating with other contractors. A shared leadership approach to this adaptive challenge would work better than a hierarchical one.

However, the tendency is to search for technical fixes to adaptive problems, and to stop there. It is easier to default to what is comfortable, what we already know. Adaptive challenges often require new skills.[26]

ADDRESSING ADAPTIVE CHALLENGES

Adaptive leadership is an iterative process involving three key activities: (1) observe the events around you, (2) interpret what you observe, and (3) design an intervention.[27] Each of these activities builds on the one that comes before it.

Fear of conflict is a major reason why many people do not exercise adaptive leadership. In the adaptive change process, conflict will arise because people are being asked to lose something they value, perhaps something as simple as a routine. It is hard to accept loss. The challenge of leadership is to work with conflict in a way that diminishes its destructive potential and harnesses its constructive energy.[28]

When people see the loss, they resist the change. They especially resist the change they don't choose. By involving people in the process, leaders can neutralize some of that resistance.[29] When people are shown how their patterns of behavior affect the system, and when people engage together to collaborate on change, they are more likely to establish a new collective identity.

Unfortunately, most organizations operate in what Edgar Schein calls "a culture of do and tell."[30] This may work when the work is technical, and the challenges are technical, but in a world of adaptive challenges, leaders need to ask and listen. In most organizations, the people in authority are expected to have the answers. It is countercultural to ask those with less status and position to solve a problem or even to provide input on the problem. As Schein points out, "Once you are above someone else, you are licensed to tell them what to do."[31]

It becomes harder to identify adaptive challenges when the culture tells managers they are supposed to already know the solution. Organizational structures, systems, and policies take root and forge cultural patterns that are hard to reshape. When things are going well, why change? It becomes hard for management to admit there are adaptive challenges.[32]

ADAPTIVE LEADERSHIP STRATEGIES

In *Leadership on the Line*, Heifetz and Linsky offer five steps for leading adaptive change: (1) get on the balcony, (2), think politically, (3) orchestrate the conflict, (4) give the work back, and (5) hold steady.[33]

1. GET ON THE BALCONY

Getting on the balcony means to look from a distance to see what is happening on the "stage floor," the place where leadership activity is occurring. Distance allows you to see yourself objectively. The balcony provides a broader view to study how you are interacting with others—and how they are interacting with each other. Getting on the balcony can help you understand the culture of your organization by seeing *how things are done around here.*

Seeing your behavior "from the balcony" is a mental exercise. It happens when you pause long enough to think about your thoughts, intentions, emotions, and behaviors and how they are impacting the thoughts, intentions, emotions, and behaviors of others. When you are practicing leadership, everything you do and say can be under a microscope. Everyone else is looking for cues as to how they should act and react.

Seeing the action and interaction from the balcony requires self-awareness and social awareness (chapter 7). The distance from the stage allows for more objectivity to see how your behaviors are affecting the actions, reactions, and interactions of others on the stage. Objectivity is only possible when you can recognize your own subjectivity.

2. THINK POLITICALLY

Thinking politically is considering the role that alliances, coalitions, and collaborative partnerships play in the process of leading adaptive change.

Because leadership involves a voluntary, interactive relationship, the process itself requires that you identify those with mutual purposes, recruit supporters to your cause, organize that support into a team, and mobilize the resources to act.

It also means being judicious about your opponents. Thinking politically includes contemplating the pros and cons of certain adaptive strategies. A power analysis helps you figure out (1) who you can count on for support, (2) who will oppose your measures, (3) who might be swayed to join you, and (4) who holds the power to enact the change. Using a political frame to view the adaptive challenge allows you to reflect on conflicting or hidden agendas, competition over scarce resources, unresolved conflicts, and the inevitable disagreements that occur in any workplace.[34]

Thinking politically about adaptive change will inevitably involve conflict because change involves loss. Asking people to lose something they care about will cause conflict.[35] The key is to inspire honest dialogue about differences of opinion, and about what needs to be done, without allowing personal disagreements to escalate into interpersonal animosity (chapter 9).

3. ORCHESTRATE THE CONFLICT

Orchestrating the conflict is like holding your hand on the thermostat of change.[36] At times, you turn up the heat to create more of a sense of urgency about the change. To increase the sense of urgency for change is to "bring the outside world in."[37] Without a sense of urgency, people lose heart.

With too much urgency, people can also lose heart. At times, you turn down the heat, so you do not burn out your people. They can feel inundated, work too fast, and make mistakes. To decrease the sense of urgency, give people time to accomplish some routine tasks. Allow more time for reflection and dialogue.

Sometimes your role is to encourage people, so they don't feel so overwhelmed, and sometimes your role is to challenge them, so they are not too comfortable with the status quo. In either case—too much or not enough urgency—some people will lose heart and may begin to resist the change. People resist loss, especially when they do not recognize the potential gains. They also resist the change they don't choose. When they are involved in choosing the change, they are more likely to buy into it. If you are experiencing lots of resistance, perhaps you need to listen more and involve people more in the process of choosing the change.

As Marty Linsky points out in the foreword to this book, adaptive leaders prepare people for the loss that invariably comes with adaptive change. When the loss experienced seems too overwhelming, the leader practices *radical empathy* to instill a sense of hope and to identify with the sacrifices people are making. When the people seem to be getting too comfortable, the leader mixes *relentless optimism* with *hard-nosed realism.*

When you are the change agent, you need to (1) ask yourself what you are asking people to give up; (2) reach out to listen to the people with the most to lose; (3) prepare people to experience some loss before they see gains; and (4) remind them of why the change is necessary and what the gains will be.[38]

4. GIVE THE WORK BACK

Giving the work back means putting the people themselves in charge of the adaptive process.[39] This can be tricky for those people in positions of authority who believe that they were hired to control everything.[40] As an adaptive leader, your job is not to *do* the work or to *solve* the problem. Doers are not necessarily leaders. Doing something, especially by yourself, can be the antithesis of leadership.

Your job is to facilitate a process where you and your team begin a dialogue with the people, especially those who are closest to the problem, and to build their adaptive capacity to change.[41] This can generate the synergy where a solution emerges that no one could have imagined by themselves.

In autocratic organizations, some people may wonder why management is consulting them. In consultative organizations, they may wonder why they are *not* being consulted all the time. When you try to give back the problem to your people, some of them might be thinking that this is the manager's job. They might wonder, "Why are you asking me? They are not paying me to do that work." It may take a while to change the culture of your organization to appreciate the consultative and participative style of adaptive leadership.

Most adaptive challenges are too complex to be led by one person, however competent that person might be.[42] Adaptive leaders involve the people closest to the problem, allow them to lead certain aspects of the change, provide them with support, and make sure everyone is working together to apply the collective wisdom of the group. In the process, leaders can become followers and vice versa.[43] People collaborate and remain in dialogue about where they are going and how to get there. Roles interchange as people seek to influence each other toward the intended changes.

5. HOLD STEADY

Holding steady means maintaining your poise in the heat of action.[44] It involves acting with character and practicing integrity, which is the basis of trust. Adaptive leaders, especially those leading change from a position of authority, must build trust so that people who see a problem are willing to speak up.[45] Adaptive leaders defend rather than squelch the voices of those who speak out for change. They insist on hearing all voices, including dissenters.

Holding steady also means sustaining disciplined attention on tough issues. People tend to slip back into long-standing behaviors unless the leader maintains focus on the brutal realities to be confronted. Adaptive leaders must identify distractions, diversions, and disruptions, and refocus on the adaptive work. Juan Carlos Eichholz says, "The more eyes and hands involved in conducting the process, the better, because there will be fewer blind spots and more mobilizing capacity."[46]

Eichholz also says, "Leadership is difficult to put into practice because it involves challenging people instead of satisfying them, asking questions instead of giving answers, generating disequilibrium and tension instead of providing comfort and safety, allowing differences to emerge instead of pretending that they do not exist, involving people instead of giving them instructions, and, in sum, confronting people with the problem instead of facing the problem by yourself or simply ignoring."[47]

MANAGING CHANGE

So far, we have been discussing the idea of *leading change*—change that is initiated through leadership. What happens when the change is dictated by an outside entity such as the government? In these cases, you are *managing the change*.

According to Heifetz and Linsky, people look to those in authority for protection, direction, and order.[48] When change is mandated from the outside, management is expected to (1) protect the interests of the organization, (2) provide direction for the change, and (3) reestablish order.

Change that is mandated from an outside entity will be enforced by that entity. The same is not true for adaptive change. Without leadership, adaptive challenges will go unnoticed and unaddressed. Without leadership, changes in the outside world are ignored as long as possible. Yes, change can occur without leadership. But leadership cannot occur without change.

CONCLUSION

Leaders for the greater good address the changes in the outside world by creating adaptive change inside their organizations. Adaptive organizations are those that evolve and align with a constantly changing environment. Adaptive leaders embrace the challenge of dealing with global change. They see conflict as a necessary part of the change process, instead of shying away from the adversity of it. They are responsive, fluid, and resilient. Ultimately, they create an organic connection to the community they serve.[49]

Adaptive challenges are leadership opportunities that present themselves daily. To become an adaptive leader, you must seize that opportunity. Only you can decide whether you lead or not. A colleague of ours, Dave Krupke, says, "When you change the way you look at things, the things you look at change." When you begin to look at adaptive challenges as opportunities for leadership for the greater good, you will discover all kinds of prospects to step up and lead.

CHAPTER 2

THE RELATIONSHIP OF LEADERSHIP

Not all human interaction involves leadership, but all leadership involves human interaction. Relationships do not define leadership, but the quality of the relationship can make or break whether the activity qualifies as leadership.

Remember that Joseph Rost provided a new definition of leadership because the old definitions did not apply to a world that had changed with the end of the industrial era. He provided his "postindustrial" definition of leadership as "an influence relationship among leaders and followers who intend real changes that reflect their mutual purposes."[1]

Influence means to make an impact, to cause an effect, or to sway someone's thinking. To qualify as leadership, the form of influence between leaders and followers cannot be coercive. The influence relationship must be multidirectional, which means the interactions between leaders and followers must flow in multiple directions—top/down, bottom/up, and peer to peer.[2]

It also means that leaders and followers can change places. People might be a leader in some relationships and a follower in others, but a leader and follower are not equal participants in the relationship. The influence relationship is unequal because leaders "are more willing to commit more power resources they possess to the relationship, and they are more skilled at putting those power resources to work."[3]

POWER

Power means the ability to act. Without power, there can be no leadership because there is no ability to change things. John French and Bertram Raven point to five sources of power: (1) coercive power, (2) reward power, (3) legitimate authority, (4) referent power, and (5) expert power.[4] The first three are more suitable for management because they require a place of authority, whereas the last two pertain more to leadership.

Coercive power is the formal ability to drive compliance, such as denying rewards or enacting punishment. *Reward* power is the formal ability to compensate, such as increasing salaries and benefits. *Legitimate authority* is the formal power to authorize and enforce organizational policies, procedures, and rules. These three are all positional sources of power.

Referent power is based on the reputation and character of the person. People *refer* to you, or identify with you, because of who you are as a person. Perhaps they admire your experience and wisdom. Perhaps it is your attention to mission and vision. *Expert* power is also based on the person. It is focused on your expert knowledge or proficiency in special areas. Because referent and expert power are personalized sources of power, they can appear with or without authority. They tend to be sources of power for leadership.

We think that *social capital* is another source of power. Social capital is established on relationships characterized by trust, loyalty, and commitment.[5] In many situations, creating change depends not only on *what* you know but *whom* you know, and how well you know them. Leaders should be very intentional about building personal relationships, not only within their team but throughout their organization, and then organizing those people into alliances.

Several researchers identified nine *influence tactics* related to French and Raven's five sources of power. Influence tactics include (1) rational persuasion, (2) inspirational appeal, (3) consultation, (4) ingratiation, (5) personal appeal, (6) exchange, (7) coalition building, (8) legitimate tactics, and (9) pressure. Research shows that the two most effective approaches are (1) inspirational appeal, which is related to referent power, and (2) consultation, which builds social capital and can be practiced with or without authority.[6]

Gaining power should be viewed as the *means toward an end* (the way to get to the result), not an end unto itself. To create change, you need power. The idea is not to build power for yourself but for the whole team, and for the purpose of creating adaptive change. If the intended change is based on mutual purposes, it is in the collective interest of the greater good. If that is the case, then the means to produce that change should also be collective. If the intended goal is to gain power simply for yourself, it is not leadership.

The paradox of power is that the more you give it away, the more powerful you can become, whereas the more you covet power, the more it corrupts.[7] This is what Mary Parker Follett means by "power with" instead of "power over."[8] When leaders and followers build power with each other, it multiplies. It is mutually owned. It is directed toward mutual purposes and intended changes. It becomes a shared power that is freely given to each other and derived from each other. In such an environment, the relationships become shared leadership, where leaders and followers do leadership together.[9]

Power can be generated by the leadership process itself. When people become *active* participants in a leadership process, they build power together and create yet more opportunities for leadership. To be active means all parties are engaged in the activities that create that power, with the intention of working toward real changes that are based on mutual purposes. Passive people do not fit the Rost definition of followership because they are not involved in the leadership process. It takes both leaders and followers to do leadership together.

Rost believes "we must learn to think of leadership as a 'communal relationship,' as a 'community of believers,' which is something larger than one leader and one follower."[10] He states that the leadership process involves more than one follower and usually more than one leader.[11] As engaged members of the leadership activity, followers do not always remain followers. They become leaders.

The fact that leaders and followers can exchange roles makes it difficult but not impossible for people in positions of authority to practice leadership. When you have authority, you cannot simply switch positions with your direct reports, rotating who is boss from day to day. Authority must be "authorized" by someone with positional power. Those without authority cannot simply decide to be the boss.

ENGAGEMENT

According to Kenneth Thomas,[12] engagement in a workplace means that the employees are "actively self-managing their work." It means that the people have *bought in* to the point where they need little or no management from the outside. Engagement relies on the intrinsic motivation of the workforce.

When the people are engaged, they are self-motivated.[13] When people are actively engaged at work, they need less management and they become more independent. When people are more independent, they become even more engaged. This becomes a virtuous cycle. With more engagement comes more productivity and less oversight. When managers spend less time supervising the people, they can pay more attention to the big picture and the people become even more productive.

Some estimates indicate that organizational cultures that place a high value on worker autonomy gain one to two hours of productive work per employee per day.[14] This is clearly in the best interest of the managers (who can spend less time supervising) and the direct reports (who are happier and healthier at work). It is also in the best interest of the organization because fewer resources must be devoted to managerial expenses.

However, research shows that about two of every three people are *not engaged* in their workplaces.[15] For a variety of reasons, most workers are just going through the motions. Perhaps they have "golden handcuffs," which means that they would like to take a different job but the money they are being paid is too much to leave that job. Perhaps they find the work is not stimulating so they do the bare minimum, working just hard enough not to be fired, but they give nothing above and beyond that. Perhaps they feel committed to the mission of the organization but think that management is not practicing what they preach.

Whatever the reason, engagement cannot be coerced. Like leadership, and like followership, it is a *voluntary* activity. As Rost points out, "Coercion is antithetical to influence relationships."[16] When people in authority overmanage or micromanage their workers, it is unlikely that workers will be willing or able to self-lead or self-manage their work. Command-and-control tactics produce the opposite. They result in overdependence, not independence. They deter engagement. At best, command-and-control methods will produce compliance.

Ralph White and Ronald Lippit studied the psychological dynamics of social organizations, presenting three styles of authority: (1) the *autocratic* approach, where all decisions are made by the persons in authority; (2) the *democratic* approach, where decisions are a matter of group discussion between workers and those in authority; and (3) the *laissez-faire* approach, where individuals are given complete freedom to make their own decisions.[17]

Leadership for the greater good requires a more democratic approach, which differs from laissez-faire because those in authority are actively involved in providing some support and direction. In the democratic approach, people in authority delegate certain responsibilities to self-led teams that have a high degree of autonomy and control over their own work, allowing leadership to emerge organically and to rotate from one task to the other. Self-led teams can train new members, assign jobs, set their own meeting agenda, assess team performance, resolve internal conflicts, and hold themselves accountable.[18]

Research shows that participation in decision-making increases engagement, which is highly correlated with worker satisfaction and productivity.[19] Engagement builds high levels of trust, commitment, and buy-in from the workers. However, engagement cannot be coerced, commanded, or controlled. It requires those in authority to consult their direct reports, involve them in decision-making, and share some of their positional power with the workforce.

INTRINSIC MOTIVATION

Research shows that to actively engage workers, those in authority need to appeal less to extrinsic rewards (or punishment) and more to intrinsic motivators.[20] Thomas identifies these four sources of intrinsic motivation: (1) meaningfulness—connecting all to a sense of purpose and direction; (2) choice—giving people some options on how to get involved; (3) competence—assigning jobs that develop the gifts and talents of the people; and (4) progress—demonstrating how their efforts are making a difference in accomplishing the *mission* and reaching the *vision*.[21]

1. *Meaningfulness*. When people are engaged, they do things for the intrinsic value of the work being done—because the work matters. They feel a higher sense of purpose about their work.[22] They can see how completing a simple task can add social benefits to something greater, such as the Merck statement: "We are in the business of preserving and improving human life."[23] They look beyond the extrinsic value of their personal reward (such as their salary) and gain intrinsic motivation.

2. *Choice*. People are more likely to be engaged when they are given choice in the matter and when their ideas and suggestions are taken seriously. Listening to workers gains their perspectives about the challenges at hand. It also engages people to buy into the process. When you are trying to lead change, people are more likely to support the change they choose, and to resist the change when they had no voice in the matter.

3. *Competence*. Involving people in the change process can provide an opportunity for them to grow. Opportunities for growth are another source of intrinsic motivators. People are more engaged in their work when they see themselves growing their skills and abilities. People in authority can recognize this and delegate responsibilities that are more rewarding to their people, thus making the work more fun and interesting.

4. *Progress*. Finally, people will be more engaged in their work when they can see incremental progress toward the intended changes based on mutual purposes. Demonstrating that today's steps are moving the group toward

tomorrow's vision of success can provide a sense of hope that is intrinsically motivating. Celebrating that progress will lift their spirits as they continue the journey toward the intended, lasting change.

SELF-DETERMINATION THEORY

Intrinsic motivation finds additional support in self-determination theory (SDT), which is one of the most developed approaches to motivation and personality. The basic notion and understanding about SDT is that human beings have natural, innate tendencies toward development of an "ever more elaborated and unified sense of self."[24]

The factors that support, or thwart, intrinsic motivation can be based on innate human tendencies. If organizations are supporting these basic human needs, then the full potential of intrinsic motivation is more likely to be actualized. The social context is crucial in determining if human potential will be unlocked or inhibited.[25] For a social environment to support the individual, it needs to take care of three needs: (1) the need for competence, (2) the need for relatedness, and (3) the need for autonomy.

Competence (which is also a factor in the Thomas model[26]) is understood as an acquired skill, such as learning to speak a new language. *Competence* refers to "feeling effective in one's ongoing interactions with the social environment and experiencing opportunities to exercise and express one's capacities."[27] The need for competence for intrinsic motivation is emphasized because it is perceived that positive feedback will encourage intrinsic motivation, while negative feedback will thwart it. The assumption is that people's competent work will be acknowledged, thus reinforcing that behavior.

Relatedness refers to "feeling connected to others, to caring for and being cared for by those others, to having a sense of belongingness both with other individuals and with one's community."[28] Although people can be intrinsically motivated by conducting a solitary activity (their example is playing solitaire), it still appears that intrinsic motivation is greater when the behavior is building social relationships.[29] We think this concept of relatedness compares well to Bass's concept of "individual consideration," one of the four *I*'s of transformational motivation (chapter 4).[30]

Autonomy (comparable to what Thomas calls "choice") means that one's actions are one's own. If someone is forcing someone to do something, or applying some type of external pressure, this would disqualify the action from being autonomous.[31] Autonomy in the context of SDT is understood as something that is originating from the person taking the action, not from someone else who is dictating what to do.[32] The general idea is that people who are functioning autonomously are more productive and are generating more wellness and human capital.[33]

As a content theory of motivation, SDT distinguishes between intrinsic motivation (doing something because it is inherently satisfying, or an end in itself) and extrinsic motivation (doing something because of some other reason than the action itself, such as a reward). Intrinsic motivation is a spontaneous tendency that elicits from someone's capabilities to develop their own personal or cognitive growth.[34] In summary, a person puts forth their full effort to support their own needs for competence, relatedness, and autonomy.

ORGANIZATIONAL CITIZENSHIP

Another concept related to engagement—one that has produced volumes of supportive research—is called *organizational citizenship behaviors* (OCBs). These include helping, participating, initiating, cheerleading, sportsmanship, and self-developing behaviors.[35]

OCBs are observable, measurable, and changeable. They are signs that the people are engaged in their work. The motivation for these behaviors comes from within the worker, not from an authority figure telling them what to do. Like leadership and followership, organizational citizenship cannot be coerced. It must be intrinsically motivated. Like engagement, organizational citizenship is based on *intrinsic motivators*.

Dennis Organ initially defined organizational citizenship as constructive behaviors that fit three criteria: (1) they are a matter of personal choice, which means not mandated by someone in authority; (2) they go above and beyond what is explicitly written in a job description; and (3) they make positive contributions to organizational effectiveness.[36]

ORGANIZATIONAL CITIZENSHIP BEHAVIORS (OCBS)

Let's say that someone has missed work for a week, and a coworker approaches that person to see how to help them get caught up. That is an OCB called "helping."

Let's say that someone sees something that needs to be done and steps up to the task without someone in authority telling them to perform that task. That is "initiating."

Let's say someone takes personal responsibility to improve the skills and abilities they need for their job. That is "self-developing."

Let's say someone is out in public and speaks highly of their organization, without being prompted. That is "cheerleading."

Research shows that these simple acts are associated with other signs of success, such as productivity, reliability, punctuality, dedication, and the accomplishment of goals. Organizational citizenship is also highly connected to the development of social capital such as trust, commitment, and cohesiveness.[37]

OCBs fit our definition of leadership and followership because they are voluntary, which means they are not mandated by those in authority. OCBs create a more constructive culture for the team or organization. Because they are intrinsically motivated behaviors, they are clear signs of engagement. Research also shows that the presence of OCBs indicates the people are ready to self-lead or to self-manage.[38]

OCB research found that *supportive* leadership behaviors would stimulate these productive workplace behaviors.[39] Research has also found some correlation between OCB and both transformational and servant leadership.[40] Transformational leadership is particularly helpful in stimulating OCB because of its focus on articulating a vision, offering a positive role model, setting high expectations and goals, and developing trusting relationships and intellectual stimulation (chapter 4).

Servant leadership can stimulate OCB because of its emphasis on recognizing the gifts and talents of others, empowering people to place those talents at the service to the organization, and placing the needs and interests of others ahead of their own.[41]

SERVANT LEADERSHIP

Servant leadership is a term coined by Robert Greenleaf.[42] In his original essay, he said that servant leadership starts with the motivation "first to serve and then to lead." The focus here is on the motivation of the leader *to serve*, which stems from a heart that is devoted to (1) the mission, (2) service to your customers, and (3) collaboration with your colleagues.

Unfortunately, many authors (not Greenleaf) have reduced the "servant leader" to being a nice person who happens to be the boss.[43] We think the servant leadership literature could be strengthened with more emphasis that (1) servant leadership is not a position, (2) servant leading includes leading change, and (3) servant leaders are powerful, although they use power as a means toward an end, not as an end unto itself.[44]

Nevertheless, we do believe that people can servant lead. If the motivation is to serve, and the intent is to generate adaptive change, and the process is voluntary and interactive, it could be described as servant leading. Dan has written extensively on this subject, insisting that servant leadership must be consistent with the definition of leadership as nonpositional.

Because it is so easy to slip into selfish motivation or narcissism, servant leadership requires faithful reflection on questions such as, *What is my motivation here? Why am I doing it this way? Is it about serving others? How does this serve the mission?* Servant leadership must emphasize the iterative process of mindful reflection and contemplative action.

The concept of service in the context of business is not a foreign one. Service adds to the authenticity and builds the credibility of the leader.[45] To paraphrase Peter Drucker, if you serve your people, they will serve your customer. If they serve your customer, the customer will be satisfied and will return for more business, and the company will be profitable.[46] Such is the paradox of altruistic service. The more you serve others, the more they will reciprocate.

Greenleaf suggests that businesses need to go beyond the typical bottom line of profitability and consider how they become social assets contributing to the greater good.[47] He criticized business schools for simply preparing students to survive and prosper within the law of the jungle, rather than teaching them to build a better society. In his view, business exists to serve society, not the other way around.

Greenleaf points to the example of George Fox, founder of the Quakers, who created a business ethic focused on honesty, dependability, and fixed prices. This built trust among his customers and allowed Quaker businesses to thrive in the seventeenth century.[48] While initially criticized for being too utopian, Fox demonstrated that ethical business can be profitable.

Greenleaf also emphasized how leaders can be searchers of truth who facilitate a process to discover the best solutions to organizational problems through dialogue, rather than pretending to have all the answers themselves.[49] He balked at the idea that ownership of a company afforded the right to command the service of others, advising those in authority to serve, rather than to be served by their workers.

Initial research shows that servant leadership can enhance intrinsic motivation and organizational citizenship.[50] It instills trust and confidence in the people being servant led. It inspires the people to participate, to take initiative, to help each other, and to develop themselves. It inspires people to go "above and beyond." It *engages* them.

We think that more needs to be researched and written about how and why fostering an attitude of service enriches the activity of leadership. It seems to us that servant leadership should naturally be part of leadership for the greater good. Unfortunately, much of what is written about servant leadership has ignored the reality of leadership as we define it in this text.

CONCLUSION

When you are leading for the greater good, people will more readily support the change if they are engaged in the change process. The way you lead (and manage) has a direct impact on the level of engagement of the people. The voluntary, interactive process we describe as leadership for the greater good will enhance the likelihood of engagement, organizational citizenship, and commitment to the adaptive change you are seeking.

Engagement is at the very heart of leadership for the greater good. To engage the people for the greater good, you must intrinsically motivate them by (1) connecting them to a meaningful sense of purpose, (2) giving them some choice in how to get involved, (3) developing their competence, and (4) demonstrating how their efforts are making progress toward accomplishing the mission and reaching the vision of the greater good.[51]

CHAPTER 3

THE ETHICS OF LEADERSHIP

APPLIED ETHICS OF LEADERSHIP

In a leadership book like this, it is possible to discuss ethics in several ways. With a purely philosophical approach, we might explore how leadership practices are associated with normative ethics.[1] We might also use a social science approach to provide a more descriptive account of the field of ethics.[2] We will use a third approach, applied ethics, and present ethical issues that can arise from the specifics of the leadership process itself.[3]

In the introduction, we stated our understanding of leadership as "a voluntary, interactive process that intends adaptive change." Our definition of leadership is consistent with Joanne Ciulla,[4] a major voice in leadership ethics who also distinguishes leadership as nonpositional and suggests that the relationship of leadership must be voluntary and interactive.

In doing so, we hope to provide more clarity to cases where there are no clear guidelines about what a morally justified course of action is. For example, where is the line between voluntary influence and manipulation? What nature of interaction is allowed? Or what type of changes would fit our ethical framework?

We will look at the ethical repercussions of a series of cases that can occur in the process of leadership. We believe the actions of trying to impress, organize, persuade, influence, and inspire people create opportunities for further ethical research. The fact that leadership should be "morally" good as well as "technically" effective makes ethics an important part of leadership discussions.[5] The types of situations we will explore include the following:

1. Ethics of people in position of authority
2. Dirty hands problem
3. Abuse of power
4. Conflict of duties

Ethics cannot be ignored in organizations for the same reasons they cannot be ignored in personal lives. Sure, there are laws and rules considered as necessary for societies to function, but there is no law that can cover every possible situation or mix of circumstances that might occur with leadership. Ethical guidelines are necessary for good functioning of society.

When we talk to our students about the ethical behaviors of their companies, we sometimes hear they are unable to make a real impact. Unfortunately, their experience aligns with research showing that almost three-fourths of education and trainings on business ethics fail to have a critical mark on business outcomes.[6] Education on ethics does impact individuals, but organizations are more than a group of individuals. While the training itself can be successful for some participants, if the organization itself does not support change through ethical policies and practices, or the people at the top of the organization are not committed to ethical change, the organizational culture does not change.

Similarly, if people in charge are not acting in alignment with ethical guidelines, no matter how many documents, seminars, and trainings, there is no reason to be optimistic about the impact of organizational commitment to ethical standards. Interestingly, there seems to be a correlation between people in positions of authority acting unethically and organizations failing. Norman Bowie,[7] a business ethicist, remarks that even a cursory glance shows a correlation between the failure of companies and the extravagant lifestyles and morally questionable behavior of CEOs and those in high positions of authority.

We believe that ethics in leadership are important for at least three reasons. First, when and if leadership is being practiced by those in authority, their actions become the public face of the organization. Second, when and if leadership is being practiced by those executives, there seems to be a correlation between their ethical choices and the performance of their companies. Finally, ethical considerations of leadership are important because organizational policies and procedures cannot cover every possible situation or version of events that can occur.

Leaders are often thought of as doing extraordinary things, shaking things up, even breaking the rules. These behaviors may be illegal and immoral and yet people considered "leaders" still act in these ways. Classic examples include the following: When is it OK to lie? Is it ever OK to motivate someone by shaming them? Is it OK to steal from the rich to feed the poor?

The "problem of dirty hands" is presented with this question: "Is it OK to violate morality in order to reach a moral goal or to bring about moral change?"[8] It is important to point out that this question does not pertain only to people in high positions. For example, a bank teller can try to improve a client's credit rating by quietly transferring small amounts of money to that person's account to get their loan approved, and then later return the "borrowed" funds to the owner's accounts.

However, these questions become even more relevant for those in high positions of authority over others. Ethical issues may arise when that positional power is being extorted for personal benefit. This can be illustrated by the "Bathsheba syndrome,"[9] named after the biblical story of the usually very moral King David, who seduced Bathsheba, a married woman, and sent her husband to be killed in battle on the front lines. When thinking of possible ways people can abuse their positional power, it seems prudent to connect ethics with leadership. Perhaps people are willing to ignore the ethical risks of following someone if they deliver the intended results, but we think it is wise to pay attention to ethical methods when bringing about any change.

Conflict of duties is another example of an ethical issue for leadership. This is an example told by our colleague Randy Richards: "Your boss calls you and the other managers together, and says, 'We are not going to be able to give people a raise this year, but I don't want anyone to know that yet. So, if anyone asks you if they are going to get a raise, tell them you don't know.' The next day one of your employees says to you, 'Hey, I was just wondering how big a raise we will be getting this year?'" It seems that no matter what people do in this situation, they are breaking some level of trust or command.

These situations not only raise doubts about the ethics of the person in question, they can raise the issue of whether the activity being considered can even qualify for leadership. Remember that the leadership relationship needs to be voluntary and interactive. Some influence tactics can become so coercive they do not qualify as leadership.

ETHICS AS A PHILOSOPHICAL DISCIPLINE

Ethics surpasses purely academic discussion because moral decisions are part of everyday human life and they are reflected in everyday questions, such as "What should I do?" On the other hand, ethics as a philosophical discipline can be described as science about morals, and it deals with human action and character.[10]

Imagine how many decisions you make during one morning: when to get out of bed, whether to take a shower, what to eat for breakfast, whether to say hello to our neighbors. When you stop at a kiosk to buy something, you are prepared to pay for the items. Most people reach those decisions without thinking about them because most are habits that need little or no conscious reflection. But occasionally, there are situations when no habits can inform your actions nor rules can steer you in the right direction. When people are faced with those situations, ethics should help make better decisions.

It is possible to distinguish at least two types of philosophical ethics: (1) descriptive ethics and (2) normative (prescriptive) ethics. *Descriptive ethics* attempts to describe behaviors, beliefs, and values. In short, descriptive ethics deals with "what things are." *Normative ethics* deals with "how things should be." The goal of normative ethics is establishing a universal system of morality. That means that (1) it is acceptable for all people and (2) it is objective.

There are at least three great traditions of normative ethics. The oldest is *virtue theory*, which searches for an answer to the question *What kind of human should I be?* Ancient Greek philosophers such as Socrates, Plato, and Aristotle belonged to this tradition. In the virtue ethics framework, human character supersedes human actions. Because of that, the basic question is not "What should I do?" but "What would a good person do in this situation?" Reframed for the context of leadership, this approach would ask, "What would a good leader do in this situation?" The "good" is defined in terms of virtues such as wisdom, humility, and kindness.

The second tradition is *deontological (or duty) theory*. This tradition points out that people are obligated to do certain things no matter what. For example, human beings should always treat others with dignity and respect. Deontological theory is based on the morality of the action itself, not the intention of the person. It offers a list of rules, such as, "Do not kill!" "Do not lie!" "Do not steal!" This theory prescribes that some actions are wrong and some are right. It is the duty of people to do the right thing no matter what. In the context of leadership, the wrong actions might include coercive influence tactics such as manipulation, intimidation, and exploitation.

The third group of theories are *teleological (or consequentialist) theories*. In this framework, there is only one criterion for right/wrong action, and it is the consequence (results) of one's action. In this manner, it is said that the action is right if its consequences are good. For consequences to be good it usually means that they increase the amount of good in the world. In the context of leadership, this tradition would calculate the pros and cons of an action based on success, such as productivity, profitability, or achievement of goals, not in terms of whether the action was morally right or virtuous.

All three theories presented here have an impact on everyday moral reasoning. They all contribute to our understanding of leadership ethics. Virtue theory suggests that character matters, especially when you consider the importance of trust between leaders and followers (chapter 2). In most cases, some deontological rules or norms, such as telling the truth and treating followers with dignity and respect, are critical to leadership. Finally, the consequences of our actions, such as the adaptive change required of leadership, needs to be considered as well.

NORMATIVE ETHICS AND APPLIED ETHICS OF LEADERSHIP

Traditionally in leadership literature, virtue ethics has been the favored approach.[11] This is not strange, since a lot of leadership literature as well as our intuitive understanding of leadership is to think about leaders as people with character. However, this approach is limited to the person who is considered the leader and not the process of leadership itself.

Concerning the teleological approach, while it does concentrate on change, or in a more general sense, on the purpose of an action (which is a necessary condition for leadership), it does suffer from the danger of justifying whatever kind of actions are necessary to achieve the desired change. For example, it is not hard to imagine people lying to their employees in order to meet a certain goal.

We think that deontological theory may be the most appropriate to offer as a guideline for leadership activities for two reasons: (1) In order to build trust, leaders need to act in a trustworthy manner. (2) In order to qualify as leadership for the greater good, leaders need to act with principle. It is their duty to influence others while treating them with dignity and respect.

For these two reasons, we propose a *categorical imperative* in the style of Immanuel Kant, who states the following: "Act only in accordance with that maxim through which you can at the same time will that it becomes a universal law." Many philosophers agree that the categorical imperative is a decision-making procedure for moral reasoning.[12] Consider the question, "Where is the line that should not be crossed when trying to influence people to commit to a voluntary, interactive process that intends adaptive change?" We think that the line is at the point where you cannot hope that your action would create a standard that could become everyone's standard in the same or similar situation.

Imagine a situation in which there are two ethical rules that state something exactly opposite and you are trying to decide what to do. Let's say that the first rule states, "It is morally right to speak the truth." The second rule states, "It is morally right to lie." What would happen if the second rule is made universal, and not the first one? Lying is possible only if it is done by the minority of people. If everybody would tell lies all the time, the very idea of truth would become invalid. It would be very hard to believe anything that anyone said. This would eventually make lying practically impossible because everybody would expect a lie.

This being the case, if an ethical rule such as "It is morally right to lie" is uplifted to the status of a universal law, the act of lying would be made impossible. Therefore, lying cannot be assumed to be morally permissible. A similar case can be made for stealing. If everybody stole, then the very idea of private property would become invalid and with it the whole concept of theft. Thus, stealing also cannot be assumed to be morally permissible. Such is the nature of a "categorical imperative." It provides a process for evaluating the activities of leadership as either fitting our ethical standards or not.

The great management guru Peter Drucker provided an example of such a moral obligation in his final book, *The Definitive Drucker*,[13] where he suggested that the best test for an organization is whether every employee could say yes to these three questions:

1. Are you treated with dignity and respect by everyone you encounter?
2. Are you provided the training and encouragement you need to contribute?
3. Do people notice your contribution?

Putting people first, ahead of profits and other signs of success, is not only the fulfillment of a categorical imperative, it is consistent with our notion of leadership for the greater good.

CONCLUSION

The deontological approach to ethics provides a useful way to evaluate the decisions and activities of leadership. We believe that leadership for the greater good requires leaders to act with principled integrity. Leaders have a duty to (1) speak the honest truth; (2) influence without coercion; (3) build trust; (4) treat others with dignity and respect; and (5) serve the needs and interests of others. These can become categorical imperatives for leadership.

When leading for the greater good, the motivation of the leader is focused on a mission, which provides a clear sense of purpose that goes beyond the pursuit of profit. Maintaining this focus can provide intrinsic motivation to the people being led. As James MacGregor Burns points out, it can raise both the motivation and the morality of the people.[14] When leaders are serving the interests of the greater good, they model behaviors that can encourage everyone to become the best versions of themselves.

PART II
THE TRADITIONAL THEORIES

INTRODUCTION

When Joseph Rost referred to the "post-industrial era," he was marking a paradigm shift that occurred when work in factories became less the norm and other, more globalized forms of business began to emerge.[1] During this postindustrial era, Rost states that leadership must become something entirely different from "good management."

As most workers moved out of factories, and as work inside factories became more technologically advanced, the practice of leadership changed but the leadership constructs did not. The definitions, descriptions, and explanations of leadership in today's textbooks have not kept pace. The realities of the postindustrial era create the need for more emphasis on *adaptive leadership* and less on the industrial theories that centered on *organizational administration*.

Let's be clear. Organizations need both leadership and management. It is not our intention here to denigrate management for the sake of glamorizing leadership. As Rost puts it, "Management, pure and simple, is necessary and essential to the good life....Devaluing management in favor of leadership has disastrous effects in the everyday life of work and play. Human beings depend on the effective and efficient management of organizations hundreds of times every day."[2]

Rosabeth Moss Kanter agrees, suggesting that most people think that management consists of rigid bureaucrats who spin red tape.[3] She states that good management allows businesses to reach specific goals on time, on budget, and in the most efficient manner. Without management, payroll is late, trains do not run on time, and the result is chaos.[4]

In this section of the book, we will present the case for leadership in the twenty-first century, without casting aspersions on management. As the pace of change in the *outside* world continues to grow, leaders need to keep pace through adaptive work that brings about change *inside* their organizations.

However, without good management to provide structure, order, protection, and smart execution, the change that leadership intends will fail.[5]

In this second section of the book, we present the traditional theories, which Rost describes as theories of the industrial age.[6] These theories are less relevant because the world has changed in these ways:

1. Fewer people work in trouble-free factories where the managers' job is simply to tell people what to do, supervise them, and motivate them extrinsically;[7]
2. Technology in the workplace, including today's factories, has become more complex, requiring managers to facilitate discussion among workers closest to the problem, and to explore solutions to technical problems, many of which are complicated with adaptive aspects as well;[8]
3. The most pressing issues tend to be *adaptive*, where problems are more complex and solutions are more elusive, requiring a new mindset for leadership and management;[9]
4. The workplace has become more diverse in terms of national and organizational culture, which further complicates the interaction between workers and managers, and among the workers themselves;[10]
5. The world has become globally interdependent, where markets and supply chains cross multiple international borders, requiring workers to coordinate, communicate, and collaborate across these borders, often using technology and online communication tools;
6. Workplace problems themselves are less stable, with the pace of change creating an unstable environment, where the adaptive issues can change before implementation of the solution even begins;[11] and
7. Things are moving so fast, and people are in such a hurry, and trying to multitask, that there seems to be less time or interest for relationship building, despite the fact that today's workplace makes those relationships ever more important.[12]

We think these global factors demand new thinking about the industrial theories of "leadership." These theories were written for a world that no longer exists. However, rather than disposing of them too quickly, we will present and interpret them in the context of a changed world. We believe that the messy complexities of today's workplace require new applications of these theories to the study and practice of leadership, something that we find lacking in the many other "leadership" textbooks we have reviewed.

In chapter 4, we will present three of the most dominant traditional approaches: transformational, transactional, and charismatic "leadership." The transformational approach, which includes charisma as one of its features, was originally written for the context of political "leadership" by Burns[13] but was later applied to business by Bass.[14] The transactional approach describes the core of management in the industrial era.

In chapter 5, we will discuss traits, behaviors, and skills as approaches that have been the focus of "leadership" studies on and off for over one hundred years. We will make the case that the traits, skills, and behaviors approaches are limited because they view "leadership" as individualistic, not as the collective, interactive, mutual influence process that is needed for today's changing world. Too often, we see lists of traits, skills, or behaviors that supposedly "define leadership," when at best, they describe and explain leadership.

In chapter 6, we will focus on situational theories and leader-member exchange theory (LMX). The situational theories are built upon the behaviors approach of the 1960s and '70s, understanding that behaviors should be conditioned by situations. In other words, what the "leader" does should depend on what the situation calls for. LMX is a more relational theory but—like the situational theories—preserves the notion that "leaders" are supervisors and "members" are their direct reports.

CHAPTER 4

TRANSFORMATIONAL, TRANSACTIONAL, AND CHARISMATIC APPROACHES

BURNS AND BASS

When we ask our students to name a great leader, they often say Mohandas Gandhi. A great example of what we teach, Gandhi engaged millions of followers around his mission. The people perceived the vision he was proposing as their own. He famously stated, "Be the change you wish to see in the world." James MacGregor Burns presents Gandhi as the quintessential example of what he calls "transforming leadership."[1]

Burns introduced transforming leadership in the context of the public arena, citing historic examples such as Gandhi and Martin Luther King.[2] Bernard Bass took Burns's idea and applied it to business, calling it "transformational leadership," which "occurs when leaders broaden and elevate the interests of their employees, when they generate awareness and acceptance of the purposes and mission of the group, and when they stir their *employees* [emphasis ours] to look beyond their own self-interest for the good of a group."[3]

With his use of the word *employees*, Bass was clearly trying to demonstrate his notion of transformational "leadership" as something that occurs in a business, and within the hierarchical relationship between a supervisor and his employees.[4]

The Bass model proposes three styles: (1) the *transactional* approach, which is what most people understand as management; (2) the *transformational* approach, which is what most people understand as "leadership"; and (3) the *laissez-faire* approach, which means that the so-called leader is not engaged, avoids making decisions, and is abdicating responsibilities.[5]

TRANSACTIONAL

"Transactional leadership" revolves around an idea that managers have resources at their disposal that they can distribute to their workers in *exchange* for their services. The relationship is based on *transactions*, which are business deals that trade a favor for a favor, that is, a *quid pro quo*, which literally means "this for that." In most cases, the transaction involves extrinsic motivators—such as rewards or punishments—that fulfill a certain interest based on exchange.

EXTRINSIC MOTIVATION

Imagine that your boss requests that you work on a certain project. A person in charge can say that if you finish this project on time you will get a certain monetary compensation. Perhaps the boss will say that if you finish ahead of time you will receive your compensation, a bonus, and on top of everything, a weekend at your favorite resort. This is an *extrinsic* form of motivation.

The Bass model presents two transactional factors based on extrinsic motivation.[6] The first is contingent reward/constructive transactions and the second is management by exception/corrective transactions.

In "contingent reward," those in authority exchange rewards for effort. They promise constructive rewards for good performance and recognize accomplishments. This is positive reinforcement, usually viewed in the form of monetary compensation. In "management by exception," the boss invokes some type of punishment or corrective discipline if the job is not done or if standards are not met.

TRANSFORMATIONAL

The Bass model presents four transformational factors based on intrinsic motivation, all of which are consistent with Abraham Maslow.[7] Often referred to as the "four *I*'s," they are (1) inspirational motivation, (2) intellectual stimulation, (3) individualized consideration, and (4) idealized influence/charisma.

Inspirational Motivation. The first factor by Bass in the transformational model is *inspirational motivation*.[8] This is about motivating followers by appealing to a deeper sense of purpose and direction. It is communicating high expectations to serve a mission and to pursue a vision. It encourages employees to act in the interest of the organization and its core values.

According to Nikolaos Dimitriadis and Alexandros Pyschogios, neuroscientific research shows that the pursuit of purpose and direction are two of the deepest longings inside the human brain.[9] When leaders appeal to mission (purpose) and vision (direction), they can enhance the ability of people to get into *flow*, which involves "moments of total absorption that lead to an optimal state of consciousness."[10] People do their best work when they connect what they are doing with a deeper sense of purpose and direction.[11] They see how their daily work is making a difference to accomplish something important to them.

Intellectual Stimulation. The second transformational factor by Bass is *intellectual stimulation*. The idea here is to challenge employees to exceed their current levels of creativity and innovation. Transformational "leaders" encourage and support their people to try new approaches and to continuously improve and develop new ways to confront issues that they are facing. They stimulate the cognitive sections of the human brain, fostering intelligence, rationality, and problem solving. They make the work fun and interesting.

Once again, neuroscientific research backs this approach. Routine problems tend to put the human brain into autopilot. What generates the full use of the human brain—and gets people into *flow*—is challenging work that requires their best gifts and talents.[12] Harnessing more capacity from the brain has become especially important in the postindustrial era, where adaptive challenges are more plentiful and even the technical problems are more complex and can demand more creative energy to solve.

Individual Consideration. The third transformational factor by Bass is *individual consideration*, which means that the "leader" nurtures a climate that supports the needs of the people and coaches them to reach their human potential. They treat each person as a unique individual. They get to know the person's needs, interests, gifts, talents, strengths, weaknesses, and preferences, so they can motivate each person with these individual characteristics in mind. They give personal attention, recognizing the dignity of each person, instead of treating everyone in the same way.

Given the growing diversity in the workplace, and the complexity that goes with that diversity, individual consideration has become even more critical to leadership. Leaders and managers need to become more adept at understanding the individual differences of people coming from various countries, religions, and cultural backgrounds. The work of Geert Hofstede demonstrates how cultural dimensions—such as individualism, masculinity, long-term thinking, uncertainty avoidance, and power distance—can help explain these human differences. Individual consideration means being considerate of the uniqueness of every individual.[13]

Idealized Influence. The final transformational factor by Bass is *idealized influence*, also known as *charisma*. Charisma evokes a strong, emotional tie between the charismatic figure (who is not always a leader) and their admirers. Charismatic persons can be strong role models. On the positive side, they can cast a vision, appeal to mission, instill pride, infuse energy, set high standards, gain respect, and build trust. They can envision, energize, and enable their people to accomplish tasks, perform effectively, and meet challenges.[14]

The most cited example we hear about this kind of influence is the great political and transformative leader Mohandas Gandhi. However, most of Gandhi's work was in the public realm. Research does not demonstrate much evidence of charisma being so important in the private business world.[15] In fact, research shows that charismatic people in business can set unrealistic expectations, create too much dependency, stifle critical thinking, take too much credit, push the blame on others, and create a sense of betrayal when things do not go well.[16]

As we will explore later, some scholars argue that idealized influence/charisma does not fit into the transformational leadership model at all.[17] They see the downside of charisma, such as the emotional impact it can have on followers to become blindly obedient and the narcissistic impact it can have on the charismatic person.[18]

THE HITLER QUESTION

Every so often, a student will ask if Adolf Hitler was a "transformational leader." Although Hitler's charismatic style does indeed qualify as idealized influence, we consider him "pseudotransformational" because he is an example of a person who uses his power for promoting his own self-interest and not for the common good.

As Peter Northouse states, the term *pseudotransformational* refers to those "leaders" who are "self-consumed, exploitive, and power-oriented," which can also be considered "personalized leadership," which focuses on the person's own interests rather than those of the group.[19]

Based on our definition, we do not consider Hitler a leader at all.

Charisma can have a mesmerizing effect on the devotees, so they become less capable of challenging the "leader" or raising contrary opinions. This can raise serious concerns for those practicing adaptive leadership. Organizational challenges today require multiple perspectives to fully understand and address them. Workers can be the first to recognize a problem, and leaders need to listen to all perspectives to identify and solve adaptive problems.

COMPARING TRANSFORMATIONAL AND TRANSACTIONAL

In all discussions on management and leadership, the issue of motivation seems to be crucial. Motivation is a drive to "move" someone and to continue that movement until the wanted result is achieved. People are motivated by many things, but with transactional (extrinsic) motivators, they do not stay motivated for as long, and they are always looking for more.

Generally, many ideas found in transformational "leadership" are supported by various theories of motivation, especially the *content* theories of motivation. The Maslow theory of motivation is an example.[20]

One of the central themes of Maslow's theory of human motivation is the concept of basic needs. According to Maslow, there are five sets of needs, which are organized in a hierarchical manner.[21] They are (1) physiological needs, (2) safety needs, (3) social needs, (4) esteem needs, and (5) self-actualization needs. The need for self-actualization is the focus for Maslow regarding leadership, management, and work-related motivation, because people are searching for meaning and purpose in their work lives.

Maslow published his notes on the subject under the title of *eupsychian management*.[22] The basic goal of eupsychian management is two-sided.[23] One is the human need for growth. The other is the organizational need to be prosperous. If management practitioners only see the second goal (prosperity of the company), then they may neglect the first goal (growth of their employees).

In short, human beings have a need "for meaningful work, for responsibility, for creativeness, for being fair and just, for doing what is worthwhile and for preferring to do it well."[24] To Maslow, humans cannot be motivated solely by pay. He argues that if their lower needs are gratified, and extrinsic rewards like money usually makes this possible, then those monetary rewards become less and less motivating. Maslow gives a few examples of intrinsic rewards that go deeper than money, such as "affection, belonging, dignity, respect, honor, appreciation, opportunities for self-actualization, and fostering of highest values (love, truth, beauty, etc.)."[25]

Frederick Herzberg builds upon Maslow's work, suggesting that money is not a "motivator" but a "hygiene factor."[26] A hygiene factor cannot increase satisfaction with a job but can only lower the dissatisfaction for that job. In other words, salaries, benefits, and other monetary rewards cannot provide long-term, intrinsic motivation. Herzberg says that true employee motivators include meaningful work, challenging assignments, participation in decision-making, personal growth, and the achievement of significant progress toward a mission.

While virtually everyone sees the need for both transactional (extrinsic rewards such as money) and transformational motivation (intrinsic rewards such as challenging work) in the workplace, the transformational approach is widely regarded as the more effective. With transactional motivation, those in authority exchange rewards for services and at best, they obtain *compliance* toward the wanted result. Herzberg would say that transactional motivators are "hygiene factors" that may get you to maintenance but not excellence.[27]

Research supports transformational motivation as the more effective approach, as it can bring about greater levels of employee engagement, dedication, and performance.[28] It can also bring out the best in others, galvanize them around a mission, and inspire them around a vision. The transformational approach intrinsically motivates people to perform "above and beyond" what is expected.[29]

CHARISMATIC

What many people commonly recognize as "leadership" is what Max Weber termed as "charismatic leadership."[30] *Charisma* in the Greek literally means "a gift from the gods," which might explain why the Greeks also thought that "leaders" were born, not made. They equated charisma with "leadership" and did not view charisma as something you developed.[31] This point has been more recently disputed.[32] The Greeks also believed that charisma gave someone the power to reign as king and ruler.

Let's be clear: not all leaders are charismatic, and not all charismatic people are leaders. If the influence process does not involve a voluntary, interactive, multidirectional relationship, then it is not the practice of leadership. Charisma is most widely used in politics, religion, sports, entertainment, and the military, but as many authors point out, not so much within business.[33]

Charisma has its advantages and disadvantages. One advantage is that it can create bursts of positive energy. The people are enthusiastic about the vision and by association, the "leader," and perhaps the organization. Charisma captivates people. They become so engrossed they are willing to do almost anything for the "leader." Charisma *can* be a gift because of how it can energize people.

Much of the work about Burns's "transforming leadership" originally focused on the study of Mohandas Gandhi.[34] Jonathan Charteris-Black also studied Gandhi, his charisma and his life, work, teachings, political activism, and communication style.[35] He concludes that one of the unique and significant parts of any charismatic person's style is communication.

GANDHI'S COMMUNICATION

Gandhi used symbolic actions. They manifested his ideology of nonviolence and showed nonviolent ways to protest and move along his agenda. By not responding to attacks, he and his followers were able to attain moral supremacy. Another technique was the use of metaphors to get his message across. He was Father, or "BAPU," to the Indian people, and his family was the whole of India. This helped to create an emotional connection between Gandhi and his followers.

He also used epigrams to capture his message in a clear and easily understandable way. One might think of them as slogans today. All these things enhanced Gandhi's ability to share his message. Since it is not possible to have one communication style that works for every audience, Gandhi did his best to cater to literate and the illiterate by different means of communication.[36]

People can learn the communication skills associated with charisma.[37] For example, people who aspire to political "leadership" can learn how to speak in a more charismatic fashion. Dan observed this personally with Barack Obama because he went through community organizing school with Obama in the 1980s. Obama went from a professional community organizer whose role was to stay behind the scenes, to a charismatic politician drawing huge crowds when he ran for president. Charismatic people excel in communication skills that can motivate and mobilize people. They hone their speaking, writing, or communication skills very carefully.

Martin Luther King inspired a civil rights movement with his sermons and speeches. He developed a cadence to his speech that is teachable. Gandhi inspired millions of people with his speaking and writing. He was able to bring his own nation to its knees by fasting almost to his death—and another nation to concede independence to India through his nonviolent efforts. Charisma can move large numbers of people. Many people have studied King and Gandhi to learn how to communicate in a more charismatic fashion.

However, there are downsides to charisma. Think of the terrible despots who have mobilized the masses to become blindly obedient. Obedience is a virtue but not when it is blind to the morals or the tactics of the so-called leader. Articulating a clear vision can be energizing but charisma can also result in a failed vision. What happens when the charismatic person misreads the signs of the times, exaggerates the situation, or is unable to detect changes in markets, politics, or culture? The persistence in a course of action by charismatic persons, and the unwillingness to listen to their own constituents, can weaken the leadership process.[38]

Charisma can create a dependent relationship between the charismatic person and the people whom Marshall Sashkin and Molly Sashkin call their "dependers," who become so enthralled with the charismatic person that they "subordinate themselves to the wishes of the leader."[39] The magical qualities of the charismatic person and the passive obedience of the "followers" creates a "seductive reciprocity" that is unhealthy and unwise.[40]

Research shows that charismatic people tend toward *narcissism*, which means they are absorbed with their own selfish interests rather than the collective will of the group.[41] Remember what happened to the Greek mythological character Narcissus, who fell in love with his reflection in a pool of water. He became so enthralled with himself that he could not leave his remarkable image, thus starving himself to death. In the same way, narcissism can have a destructive effect on the leadership process.

We think that "charismatic leadership" is overrated. In most cases, it is not even leadership. Granted, it can generate lots of energy for the vision of the charismatic person, but it has serious downsides. Rare are the examples of charismatic people who are dedicated to serve instead of being served. As charismatic people grow in fame, the praise and loyalty that mounts can be a huge obstacle to the practice of leadership for the greater good. It takes great self-awareness to maintain humility in the face of such popularity.

Strength of character is more important than personal magnetism.

CONCLUSION

All four of the transformational factors (the four *I*'s) add value to our understanding of leadership for the greater good. They suggest higher attention be paid to intrinsic motivation, engagement, and communication. They remind us that leading for the greater good should be (1) inspirational, (2) individually considerate, (3) intellectually stimulating, and (4) idealistic. The idea is to transform people, teams, and organizations, and to transform followers into leaders. Ultimately, this approach could embolden the transformation of society.[42]

As for the case of Gandhi, his example teaches that leaders must act with integrity, making sure that what they do is aligned with what they say.[43] His example can also teach us about how a virtuous life can be the remedy to the narcissistic tendencies of a charismatic person. To lead change for the greater good, you must consciously reflect on when you are acting on purely selfish motives and when you are acting in the best interest of the mission, the team, and the organization.

CHAPTER 5

TRAITS, BEHAVIORS, AND SKILLS

THE PROBLEM

Books that sell at airport bookstores often herald the "eight essential traits," "six sure-fire behaviors," or "nine necessary skills" to become a "leader." The assumption is that if you develop a certain set of traits, or practice a specific set of behaviors, or refine certain skills, you will be a "leader"—whether you are involved in a voluntary, interactive relationship that is changing things or not.

We agree that there are certain traits, behaviors, and skills associated with best practices in leadership. However, most of them are not unique to leadership. They could apply equally to management—or to a variety of other activities, such as teaching, parenting, or coaching. For example, we might say that leaders are humble (a trait), ask good questions (a behavior), and practice good listening skills. However, we could also make the case that humility, asking, and listening correspond likewise to managing, teaching, parenting, or coaching.

Managers, teachers, parents, and coaches can and do practice leadership at times. However, they are not leaders per se. Leadership is not ex officio. Practicing leadership does not happen simply because you hold a title or position. Nor do you become a "leader" just because you hold certain qualities, display certain behaviors, or practice a set of skills. You exercise leadership when you influence others to join you in a voluntary, interactive relationship that intends adaptive change.

Traits portray individual characteristics. Behaviors depict certain actions. Skills are specific behaviors that have reached a level of proficiency. Traits, behaviors, and skills can help to *describe* and *explain* leadership. None of them *define* leadership.

THE TRAITS APPROACH

More than one hundred years ago, the historian Thomas Carlyle famously stated that "the history of the world was the biography of *great men* [italics ours]."[1] His "great man theory" assumed that "leaders are born" with a set of divinely endowed traits that explain their secret to heroic success. Historians like Carlyle identified famous men (excluding women), assumed they were "leaders," and tried to glean what set of traits made them successful. They figured that if people wanted to become "leaders," they just needed to adopt the traits of these famous men. They concluded that these all-male "leaders" were superior because they were tall, strong, courageous, intelligent, and masculine (imagine that).

In 1948, Ralph Stogdill reviewed 124 different studies on traits and discovered some patterns that might explain "leadership."[2] He found that "leaders" tended to be more extroverted, intelligent, dominant, responsible, adaptable, ambitious, persistent, and confident than the average person. After finding no statistical significance in his data, Stogdill concluded that "leadership is not a matter of passive status or of the mere possession of some combination of traits."[3] He switched his research focus to behaviors, which are more observable, measurable, and changeable than traits. (We will review behaviors below.)

In 1991, Shelley Kirkpatrick and Edwin Locke proposed a "modern" approach to trait theory, with several key traits they considered "pre-conditions" to "leadership":[4]

- Drive (motivation to "lead")
- Self-confidence
- Honesty (integrity)
- Intelligence (cognitive)
- Knowledge of the business

The first two—drive and confidence—can certainly explain why some people take the initiative to "lead" while others do not. Drive and confidence can fuel the passion that is needed to initiate change and sustain the efforts of "leadership." Honesty is the foundation of trust and has been highlighted as crucial to "leadership" in many studies.[5]

The final two—intelligence and knowledge of the business—are also on many "leadership" trait lists. However, research by Goleman and others show that EQ (the measure of emotional intelligence) is more critical than IQ (the measure of intelligence—more on that later too).[6] Knowledge of the business can be helpful at entry levels of management but less important in higher levels of management.[7] In fact, too much knowledge of the business can distract senior and middle managers from seeing the big picture and can foster micromanagement.

One could argue that *too much* of certain qualities can be just as detrimental as too little. For example, too much drive, ambition, and desire could produce such high expectations that they wear out those around you. Too much self-confidence can appear to be arrogant and is sometimes associated with narcissism. Too much intelligence can result in less patience with others who take longer to figure things out.

In 2002, a meta-analysis of "leadership studies" explored the relationship between "leadership" (identified mostly through hierarchical rank) and the "Big Five" personality factors: (1) extroversion, (2) conscientiousness, (3) openness, (4) agreeableness, and (5) freedom from neurosis.[8] Results found significant correlation between "leadership" and all five factors except agreeableness. Extroversion had the strongest association.

In 2004, the same authors conducted another meta-analysis of "leadership studies."[9] This time, they explored the relationship between "leadership" and *intelligence*, given that intelligence had often appeared as a significant correlate in various studies. What they found was a modest correlation, but "considerably lower than previously thought." Unfortunately, a close look at their research methods reveals that most studies identified their "leaders" as people in positions of authority. In our view, this qualifies the results as interesting to good management but not so much to the activity of leadership.

James Kouzes and Barry Posner have produced some of the best research and writing on both traits and behaviors over six editions of their classic book *The Leadership Challenge*.[10] They identified their sample by asking people to name individuals who they viewed as "exemplary leaders" in their organization—which is an improvement from simply studying people in authority and calling that "leadership." The four traits they found most significant were (1) honest, (2) forward-looking, (3) inspiring, and (4) competent.[11]

To be *honest* is to be trustworthy, that is, worthy of someone's trust. We have discussed this Kouzes and Posner list of traits with thousands of our students. Just about everyone agrees that when looking at traits of an "exemplary leader," *honesty* (integrity) is the most important. After all, honesty is the basis of trust. In order to build trust, a leader must act in a trustworthy manner. Trust is the foundation of all collaborative relationships, including leadership.

To be *forward-looking* is akin to being strategic about the future. Many of our students view forward-looking as the trait that is most unique to the activity of leadership. We agree that leaders need to look forward in order to anticipate adaptive changes. Nevertheless, we can also make the case that managers and followers also need to be forward-looking. All members of the team should be involved in the process of envisioning the change.[12]

To be *inspiring* is akin to inspirational motivation, which is a factor in the Bass transformational model (the four *I*'s).[13] The word *inspire* means "to breathe" new life, to motivate someone from within their spirit. Appealing to mission and vision can inspire, animate, energize, or intrinsically motivate the people. Inspiring is a form of influence that can occur with or without a position of authority. It can also occur inside or outside the activity of leadership.

To be *competent* means "to be fit," to be able, to be prepared to take on a certain job. Competence is an important trait but is not unique to leadership. Workers, managers, and everyone else needs to be competent. Of course, competence is important to leadership, but it is quite rare to see it included on lists of traits specifically associated with leadership.[14]

TRAITS OF LEADERS AND FOLLOWERS

We have noticed that most of the "leadership" traits identified on these lists could be just as likely to describe good "followership." A classroom exercise we use illustrates this point. We divide our students into two groups, asking one group to develop a list of traits of the "ideal follower," and the other to develop a list of traits of the "ideal leader." Imagine their surprise when they develop nearly identical lists.

It should be no surprise because if leadership is viewed as an interactive process involving leaders and followers who influence each other, both roles require similar traits, behaviors, and skills. If leaders and followers can exchange positions, as Rost suggests, then the two functions are inseparable.[15] Followership becomes training for leadership.[16]

Scholars have not been able to find any validity to one set of traits that can define, measure, or predict the presence of "leadership." Nevertheless, the study of traits is not a useless activity. While it cannot define, measure, or predict leadership, it can be useful to *describe the people* involved in leadership—and followership.

Traits can be viewed as the flip side of behaviors. For example, honesty is a trait associated with behaviors like telling the truth, modeling exemplary behavior, and practicing what you preach. Being forward-looking is a trait associated with behaviors like planning strategically, thinking creatively, and anticipating adaptive change. When we coach our students to think about improving their leadership, they often start by identifying traits to work on—and then they identify the behaviors associated with that trait.

THE BEHAVIORS APPROACH

The behavioral approach to "leadership" focuses on "what leaders do."[17] The main advantage of this approach is that behaviors are observable, measurable, and changeable. They are more concrete. The study of behaviors is considered a sociological approach, while the study of traits is considered a psychological view.

One early study of behaviors distilled 1,800 statements on "leadership" to derive two general categories of behavior: (1) the task, which was initially called "initiating structure," with its focus on providing direction and control, and (2) the relationship, which was initially called "consideration," with its focus on providing support and concern for people.[18]

Initially, these behaviors were measured on a one-continuum, ten-point scale between task and relationship (chart 3). A lower score was more task-oriented, while a higher score signified more attention to the relationship. Inventories were created to score people on this single continuum.

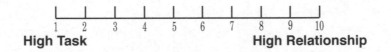

Chart 3: Task vs. Relationship

When we ask our students to identify themselves on this scale of one to ten, most can quickly identify their behavioral tendencies. The next question we ask them is to name the situations that might move them in one direction or the other. For example, even the most relationship-oriented person might become more task-driven when facing a deadline. That is why situational theories later emerged out of the behaviors approach (chapter 6).

However, the ten-point model in chart 3 assumes that every step a person takes to get the job done represents one step away from building relationships. And vice versa. The model mistakenly pits task and relationship as opposing ends of one continuum. This presents them as a *false dichotomy*, which is a choice posed as either/or when the choice is not mutually exclusive.

Task and *relationship* can be viewed as the yin and yang of all human behavior, including leadership and management. In Chinese philosophy, the yin and yang describe a dualism that exists when seemingly opposite forces are complementary, interconnected, or perhaps interdependent. The yin and yang give rise to each other. Natural dualities such as male and female, light and dark, fire and water are examples of the yin and yang. For example, the male cannot exist without the female, or vice versa.

It is hard to imagine a relationship that is completely divorced from a task—or a task that is totally separated from a relationship. Completing a task can forge a relationship. Building a relationship can hasten the completion of a task. The task and relationship are reciprocal forces that complement each other. Together, they form a whole that is greater than either part.

The "managerial grid," presented by Robert Blake and Jane Mouton in 1964, took a different approach to this duality and posed task and relationship as two complementary factors, each on its own axis (chart 4).[19]

The (1,9) approach is *high task/low relationship* behavior. It focuses on directing and controlling the activities of the workers but has low concern for relationships.

The (9,1) approach is *high relationship/low task*. It involves creating a comfortable, friendly work environment but has low concern for production.

The (1,1) approach is *low task/low relationship* behavior. It depicts behavior that shows neither concern for work getting done nor concern for the workers.

The (5,5) approach shows *medium* levels of concern for people and production.

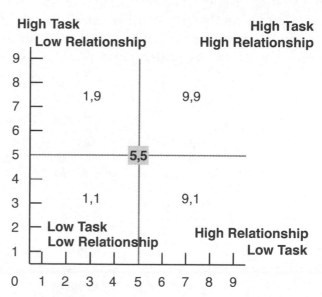

Chart 4: The Managerial Grid by Blake and Mouton

The (9,9) approach is a *high task/high relationship* orientation. It is considered by many as the ideal style, with high levels of direction and support.

In 2004, a team of researchers conducted a meta-analysis of studies on *consideration* (the relationship) and *initiating structure* (the task).[20] They found that consideration was strongly related to motivation of the worker, effectiveness of the manager, and job satisfaction for both manager and direct reports. Initiating structure was positively related to the effectiveness of the manager and to the performance of the organization.

It is important to note that in these studies, most of the people studied were people in positions of authority. With this in mind, we find that most of the lessons to be learned from the behavioral approach are applicable to management, or to the practice of leadership when you are also managing. Nevertheless, some useful management training programs have emerged out of this research on task and relationships, one of which we will review next.

Q4 LEADERSHIP

Psychological Associates developed a training program called *Leadership through People Skills* that is based on high levels of concern for the task and the relationship.[21] They measure *assertiveness* on the task vertically and *warmth* on the relationship horizontally, providing four behaviors depicted in chart 5. This model of human behavior, with its four emerging styles, can be applied to leaders, followers, managers, and direct reports.

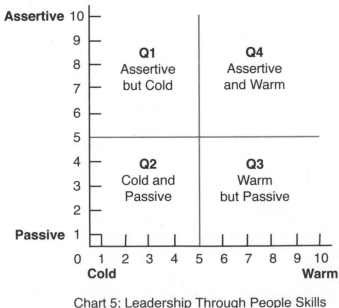

Chart 5: Leadership Through People Skills
© by Psychological Associates

Q1 behavior (which is comparable to 1,9 in the Blake and Mouton model) is cold (on the relationship) and assertive (on the task). It provides direction but not support, showing little regard for the needs of others. This behavior especially typifies dominant bosses who have a clear sense of how to solve problems but do not invite the input of others. Perhaps they lack the confidence, patience, or humility to be consultative. For whatever reason, they do not consider the viewpoints of others. They tell but do not ask.

Q2 behavior (comparable to 1,1) is passive (on the task) and cold (on the relationship). At its worst, this is *passive-aggressive* behavior. A lot of Q2 behavior can be attributed to the surrender that comes from dealing with prolonged Q1 behavior, especially from a boss.[22] When a person gets commanded, controlled, and confronted with repeated Q1 behavior, they tend to feel defeated. They can regress into Q2 behavior.

Q3 behavior (comparable to 9,1) is warm (on the relationship) but passive (on the task). As a managerial approach, it provides support without direction, allowing people to do whatever they want, much the same as the *laissez-faire* approach (although with more support).[23] Sometimes, Q3 behavior is an attempt to get others to like you. If that is the case, and you are such a people pleaser, it might help to remind yourself that if the people are committed to the mission (the task), they will be more "pleased" when they see progress toward that mission.

Q4 (comparable to 9,9) is the optimal approach.[24] It is highest in concern for the task *and* the relationship. It is assertive (on the task) and warm (on the relationship) at the same time. It is the ideal behavior for leaders, followers, managers, or direct reports. To act with Q4 is to be assertive, confident, and passionate about the mission while also collaborative, considerate, and supportive of others in the pursuit of that mission.

Q4 behavior fits well with our definition of leadership and followership. To be engaged in a voluntary, interactive relationship that builds trust requires high regard for the relationship. To be actively seeking adaptive change requires high regard for the task. The Q4 model provides a useful way to think about what behaviors are most appropriate for adaptive leadership.

THE QUADRANTS DESCRIBE BEHAVIOR, NOT PEOPLE

Imagine that you are promoted to be director of your department. With each decision you make, with every conversation you engage, with every situation you address, you have a choice to be either dictatorial (Q1), passive-aggressive (Q2), agreeable (Q3), or collaborative (Q4). While there is a tendency with this model to characterize certain people as always Q1, Q2, Q3, or Q4, the reality is that people move in and out of these behavioral styles throughout the day. The model describes behavior, not people.[25]

THE FIVE PRACTICES OF EXEMPLARY LEADERSHIP

Model the Way

1. Set an example by acting with integrity.
2. Achieve small wins that show progress toward the mission.

Inspire a Shared Vision

1. Envision an exciting future.
2. Enlist others to make it a shared vision.

Challenge the Process

1. Search out challenging opportunities to grow.
2. Experiment, take risks, and learn from experience.

Enable Others to Act

1. Foster collaboration and trust.
2. Strengthen others to get the job done by providing resources and support.

Encourage the Heart

1. Recognize individual achievements by thanking people.
2. Celebrate team accomplishments.

Chart 6: Five Practices of Exemplary Leadership by Kouzes and Posner

Kouzes and Posner have been researching traits and behaviors of "ideal leaders" for over thirty years.[26] Their five practices, which were identified through a factor analysis from thousands of cases of "exemplary leadership," are illustrated in chart 6. The five behaviors can be measured with an instrument, called the *Leadership Practices Inventory* (LPI), which is one of the most widely used leadership/management assessments in the world.

The LPI, which has been included in hundreds of research projects, and used by tens of thousands of people, includes thirty items, six of which match up with each of the five practices. A quick look at these thirty items can give anyone a snapshot of how well they are leading and managing along these five practices (see www.leadershipchallenge.com).

Many businesses use the LPI as a 360-evaluation tool. Individuals being scored fill out the LPI (with its thirty items), and so do several people who know them, including their boss, direct reports, and peers. For the most honest results, the LPI should be used as a tool for coaching (not for performance evaluation). It is designed for personal and professional development. If used as an evaluation tool, the scores may be skewed to protect or to attack the person being scored.[27]

We have used this instrument many times in our leadership and management coaching, as we have in the classroom. It is a useful tool to identify areas for growth and development. The people being scored should identify which practices they want to focus on, and with coaching, develop strategies for improvement.[28]

Chart 6 lists the five practices and ten behaviors of "exemplary leadership."[29] With each practice, the authors describe two more specific behaviors, one that is a more individual step and the second that is more collective. The first involves more of an inward step toward that practice; the second is more of an outward step associated with that practice.[30]

To *model the way* means to be clear about your values, to practice what you preach, and to live with integrity in everything you say and do. This is essential to building trust, which is the foundation of all leadership activity. The practice also includes recognizing how the organization can live out its mission and corporate values.

To *inspire a shared vision* begins with envisioning the future yourself, being clear about the change you want to lead. The second part of this practice is cocreating a sense of "shared vision" (not just yours but one that is shared mutually). This means facilitating a process where the group identifies adaptive challenges, explores solutions, listens to each other, and develops strategies to move toward the future (chapter 10).

To *challenge the process* is to open your mind and heart to the possibility of change, to challenge the status quo, and to seek new opportunities. It also means working with your team to try new approaches to solving adaptive challenges, to experiment with new strategies, including ones that might be risky, and then to learn and grow from your success and failures.

To *enable others to act* starts with developing collaborative and trusting relationships, and then strengthening those relationships by assuring that the people you lead or manage have the support and direction they need to accomplish the mission.

To *encourage the heart* begins with nurturing a sense of gratitude within yourself, bringing a positive attitude to the team and showing your gratitude for individual members on a regular basis. It also means taking the time to celebrate meaningful milestones as a team.

Instead of assuming all people in positions of authority are leaders, as most research does, Kouzes and Posner asked people in organizations to identify colleagues who they considered to be an "exemplary leader." This allowed for the possibility that some of their research subjects were people without positional authority.[31]

We think that the five practices of the Kouzes and Posner model provides another useful way for leaders and followers to think about practical behaviors that can build voluntary, interactive relationships, such as modeling the way and encouraging the heart. The model also suggests ideal ways to organize adaptive change, such as challenging the process and inspiring a shared vision. The fifth behavior, enabling others to act, seems to be a good model for managing during an adaptive change process.

THE SKILLS APPROACH

Skills are another way to think about behaviors. Skills are specific behaviors that have been practiced to proficiency. Identifying skills needed for employment is a typical job for human resource managers. Identifying skills needed for leadership can be another way to discern preparation for leadership.

We will explore dialogical, emotional, conflict, and strategic skills in the final four chapters of this book. Before doing so, we will review a popular model originated by Robert Katz in 1955.[32] While it describes management in the industrial era, it still has some relevance to the realities of adaptive work in today's business environment.

According to the Katz model,

1. Technical skills are most important at the lowest levels of management.
2. Conceptual skills are most important for senior management.
3. People skills are moderately important at all levels.

When a person is first hired and is expected to supervise front-line workers, the Katz model suggests that he or she relies most heavily on *technical skills*, or knowledge of that business. For example, in a John Deere manufacturing facility, front-line supervisors need to know about axles, transmissions, and gear boxes used in tractors, combines, and other heavy equipment. Those who manage closest to the actual production, or to the service being provided, need to understand the technical side of the job.[33]

As people are promoted into middle management, the Katz model suggests that they rely less on technical skills and begin to rely more heavily on *conceptual* skills. They begin to see the bigger picture and make contributions toward setting the strategy, revising the structure, and nurturing the culture of the organization. According to Katz, people skills are still moderately important in middle management, as people are asked to "manage up," "manage down," and "manage sideways."[34]

In the Katz model, "senior managers" are required to excel at the conceptual side of the business, such as strategic planning, decision-making, and market forecasting. The model suggests they need little technical knowledge of the business. In fact, having a technical view can sometimes distort the strategic view that is so critical at the senior levels of management.[35]

From our perspective, the Katz model has some value for suggesting what skills are most necessary as *managers* are promoted. It makes sense that those supervisors who are closest to the actual work would need the most technical skills, and those at the top need the most conceptual skills. We also think that as the workplace becomes more automated, and as communication becomes more remote, the need for *technology* skills will surge. This is not the same as the *technical* skills specific to making goods or providing services of one certain company.[36]

Most importantly, we think the Katz model underestimates the importance of people skills. Given the growing amount of diversity in the workplace, the growing need for collaboration to do adaptive work, and the growing use of online communication in the workplace, we think that people skills have become even more critical for leadership and management. We think they are the most important set of skills at all levels of management. While technical skills are often considered the "hard skills" and people skills are referred to as the "soft skills," we believe that people skills are the "hardest skills."

If companies are interested in doing adaptive work, and especially if they wish to move toward self-led and self-managed teams, the need for cognitive skills has also become more important in the postindustrial era, especially problem-solving, critical thinking, and innovation skills. In fact, being able to notice trends in the business, seeing the big picture, and identifying adaptive changes are critical skills at all levels of the organization.

The Katz model provides a paradigm for reflecting upon the three areas of skills that are needed in leadership and management. It has survived the test of time with its insight into the skills needed for management, and how the need shifts as a person is promoted from entry levels of management to senior levels. We think the model still has some applicability, especially in very large organizations where there are multiple layers of management.

CONCLUSION

When coaching someone in leadership for the greater good, it is helpful to identify traits, behaviors, or skills that can fit into a plan for personal development.

However, most of the lists that are reviewed in the dominant literature were created in the industrial era. They need fresh interpretation to determine their usefulness in today's business environment. The research conducted in traits, behaviors, and skills usually identify "leaders" in hierarchical terms. They use language that assumes that the "leader" is a boss or supervisor.[37]

Nevertheless, we think that an introduction to leadership theory would be incomplete without considering some of the insights that research on traits, behaviors, and skills have provided. We find the five practices of exemplary leadership by Kouzes and Posner to be particularly useful and consistent with our notion of leadership for the greater good.[38] We highly recommend the use of the Leadership Practices Inventory as a tool for leadership coaching and self-improvement.

CHAPTER 6

SITUATIONAL THEORIES AND LMX

FOUNDATION OF THE SITUATIONAL THEORIES

Situational theories are based on sociological research that prefers to study behaviors. The early behavioral theories were inspired by Douglas McGregor's Theory Y, which assumes that people are basically good, and that given the proper amount of (1) direction and (2) support, people will thrive without command-and-control techniques.[1]

At issue is the following: What is that proper amount of direction and support? What situations call for what mix of direction and support? Which situations require greater direction and which ones require greater support? What is the best fit between the situation and the behavior?[2]

The situational model of Paul Hersey and Kenneth Blanchard builds upon Blake and Mouton's "managerial grid,"[3] where behaviors fall into two categories: (1) those providing *direction*, which are motivated by "concern for production," which we will refer to as *the task*; and (2) those providing *support*, which are motivated by "concern for people," which we will refer to as *the relationship*.

Situational theories present a different viewpoint than the Q4 model, which teaches that the situation *always* calls for high task and high relationship behavior.[4] Situational theories suggest that certain situations demand more direction while others call for more support. The situational models also assume that the "leaders" or managers *can* change their behavior based on what the situation calls for.

SITUATIONAL LEADERSHIP THEORY

What is called "situational leadership" (SL) was written in the industrial era and it assumes that the "leader" has positional authority. However, it has certain strengths that can enlighten those trying to manage or lead from a position of authority. It is still taught in corporate trainings all over the world.

SL posits four situational behaviors, each based on some combination of concern for the task or concern for the relationship: (1) telling, (2) selling, (3) participating, and (4) delegating (chart 7).[5] The original theory (SLI) was later updated by Ken Blanchard in 1985, to situational leadership II (SLII), in which the names of the behaviors were changed to (1) directing, (2) coaching, (3) supporting, and (4) delegating. For our purposes here, we will use the language of the original version (SLI).

The theory offers one situational factor that determines which of four behaviors is best for each scenario. That one independent variable is the *readiness* (R) level of the follower, measured as either R1 (willing but unable), R2 (unwilling and unable), R3 (unwilling but able), and R4 (ready, willing, and able). These four readiness levels of the follower line up with the four situations (S1, S2, S3, and S4) in chart 7.

(S1) *Telling* is used by this theory to describe behaviors that are high task, low relationship. This approach is most appropriate when the presenting behavior of the followers is R1. This means they are not ready to do the job because, while they feel some *confidence* as new to the task (willing), they are not yet *competent* (able) to do the job. In this type of situation, the model suggests that the supervisor should tell the other person what to do.

From our perspective, telling might make sense, but only when (1) the person who is telling knows the answer, and (2) the person being told does *not* know the answer. If either, or both, of these factors is not the reality, it makes more sense to *ask* than to tell. Excessive telling is a traditional management technique of the industrial era.[6] It is part of the yesteryear mindset that needs to change. Telling works best when problems are technical in nature, when the teller knows the solution, and when the person being told does not already know what is being told.

In the industrial era, when jobs might have been as simple as putting hubcaps on vehicles, and something went wrong, the supervisor on the assembly line knew what to do and could tell the worker what to do. However, in this

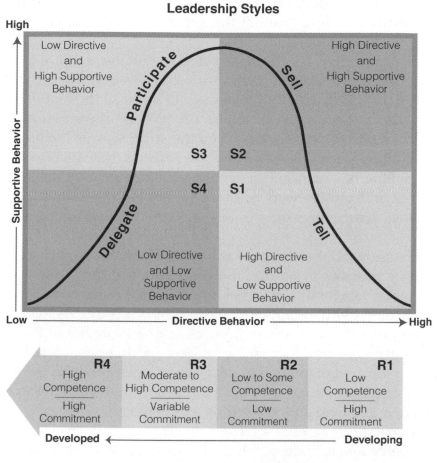

Leadership Styles

Chart 7: Situational Leadership I (SLI)
by Hersey and Blanchard

postindustrial era, the adaptive issues are more complex, and even the technical problems are often difficult to solve. What is needed is more asking, listening, and dialogue with those closest to the problem.

(S2) *Selling* is described in this theory as high-task, high-relationship behavior. It is most appropriate when the presenting behavior of the worker is R2, where the person is neither willing nor able to do the job. In this situation, the model suggests that the supervisor use the highest measure of both task (directive) and relationship (supportive) behavior and sell their idea. The subtle difference between telling and selling is important here.

In this second phase of readiness, the worker needs highly supportive behavior (because the worker lacks confidence) and highly assertive behavior (because the worker also lacks competence). The influence process is less

---

authoritarian and more persuasive than was the case in S1 (telling). The basic idea in this part of the model is that the supervisor sells his or her idea to the point where the worker buys in.

From our perspective, it does make sense that when workers are not willing and not able, that you approach them with behaviors that are high relationship (to address the unwillingness) and high task (to address the inability). However, the model assumes the supervisor knows the answer, the solution, or the best way to perform a job. What happens when the supervisor is "selling" the wrong answer? What happens if the worker sees something that the boss misses? The approach of selling is somewhat better than telling because the boss is trying to get some buy-in from the worker. But according to this model, what is being "sold" is an idea that comes only from the supervisor without input from the worker.

In the postindustrial era, where the work is more complex and the challenges are more adaptive in nature, the best ideas will not always emerge from those in authority. Leadership on these issues is not limited to those with supervisory responsibility. With adaptive challenges, it is more advisable to convene a team that can present multiple perspectives on the issue, identify the problem, explore solutions, generate new ideas, and act on them. Such is the nature of leading change for the greater good—not "selling" the people on the supervisors' ideas. It is cocreating new ideas that emerge out of dialogue characterized with *more asking and listening* and less telling and selling.[7]

(S3) *Participating* is characterized in this theory as low-task, high-relationship behavior. It is considered most appropriate when the presenting behavior of the worker is R3. This means that the person is feeling more capable of doing the task (able) but has lost confidence that he or she can do it (not willing). In this situation, the model suggests that the supervisor uses the lowest measure of task behavior (to address the higher level of competence of the worker) and the highest measure of supportive behavior (to address the lower level of confidence of the worker). This is described as "participating." The basic idea here is that the supervisor allows the other person to participate in the decision-making and problem-solving process.

From our perspective, there is some common sense to this part of the theory. As a worker becomes more capable of doing the job, but perhaps is less willing than before, it is suggested that the boss should sit down with that person and decide together how to approach a problem or perform a task. We agree with the participative approach and think it ought to be considered in the two previous situations as well. The people who are closest to a problem have a unique perspective on how to identify and solve adaptive problems. Generally, the more they weigh in on the problem, the better the solution, and the more likely they are to buy into that solution.[8]

In a world where most problems are adaptive in nature, or where even the technical problems are more sophisticated, it is important to maximize participation when identifying, analyzing, planning, and deciding how to address challenges. However, we believe a participative approach is not necessarily "low-task" behavior (less assertive). We believe that when those in authority involve their workers in identifying problems and discovering solutions, they should be *assertive* about their own ideas while *cooperative* about the ideas of others. This is Q4 behavior—which is high task and high relationship (chapter 5).

(S4) *Delegating* is considered low-task, low-relationship behavior. The model presents it as most appropriate when the presenting behavior of the worker is R4. This means the worker is ready, willing, and able to do the job—by themselves. In this type of situation, the model suggests that the supervisor uses the lowest measure of task and the lowest measure of relationship behaviors because the other person is fully ready to do the job on their own.

Note that the level of "support" in this section of the model never goes to zero (chart 7). The idea is that delegation is not dumping.[9] Delegation requires feedback and support. Delegation means "to send someone on a commission." It is not just a way to clear your desk of tasks you do not want. It does not mean asking someone to make certain tasks disappear from your to-do list. Delegation is a means of developing the leadership potential in others. The opposite of micromanagement, delegation allows the other person to develop their own gifts and talents, often learning through their own mistakes.

When considering delegation as an opportunity for leadership, it is important to find a good fit between the needs of the organization and the talents of the person to whom you are delegating the task. In chapter 8, we will discuss humble inquiry and how it can help you determine who is fit for delegation and how to provide the support people need.[10] The human tendency is to do things by yourself instead of spreading the work around. Doing something by yourself might give you more control but it is not leadership. It also limits the amount and quality of work that can be done, and the number of people who feel ownership of the work.

Delegation can be the ultimate compliment to someone who is ready, willing, and able to do the job. It shows that you have full confidence in their ability to perform and they no longer need your directions. However, the adaptive challenges people face today cannot be conquered by one person, even if that person has many gifts and talents. It makes sense to delegate some responsibility to others, but they will need a team around them to address adaptive change.

We believe that when delegating responsibility to an R4 (who is ready, willing, and able to take on the task), the delegator ought to allow the delegate to *lead* change, not simply to *manage* it. That means empowering the change agent to take the initiative, not to take directions from above. When people have progressed to R4, it would be a good opportunity to set up a *self-led team* where leaders and followers can exchange positions.[11]

Leading *with* authority can mean quietly taking a back seat, but not leaving the room. Most adaptive challenges are going to need the people in authority to be present to provide feedback and support—but not to dictate the terms of action. This takes wisdom to know you do not have all the answers, and humility to admit to others that you do not have all the answers.

Situational theory can provide helpful insights into how to approach a team with the right mix of directive and supportive behaviors. We believe it presents some insights for "good management." Weaknesses of the theory include assumptions that (1) the supervisor has the ability to change his or her behavior as the situation dictates; (2) the supervisor knows best what he or she should tell or sell when the situation dictates; and (3) the readiness level of the follower is the only variable for deciding between the four behaviors.

Many other factors ought to be considered when deciding whether to tell, sell, participate, or delegate. These might include (1) the urgency and importance of the task; (2) the urgency and importance of the relationship; (3) the readiness level of the manager; (4) the complexity of the task, such as the level of technical versus adaptive nature of the challenge; (5) the amount of time and resources available; and (6) the structure and culture of the organization. Some of these factors are considered in the path-goal theory.

PATH-GOAL THEORY

Path-goal theory recognizes that the behavioral response of the supervisor (they say "leaders," but the theory assumes positional authority) is dependent on many factors, not just the readiness level of the worker. Robert House and Terrence Mitchell suggest that the correct behavioral approach by the manager will *clear the path* so that the worker can *reach the goal*; thus, the "path-goal" theory.[12] It considers the right mix of task and subordinate characteristics, which determine what supervisory style would best fit a situation in order to improve the motivation of the workers.

Managers adopt different behaviors depending on the variation of the task and worker characteristics.[13] The four manager behaviors are (1) directive, (2) supportive, (3) participative, and (4) achievement oriented.[14]

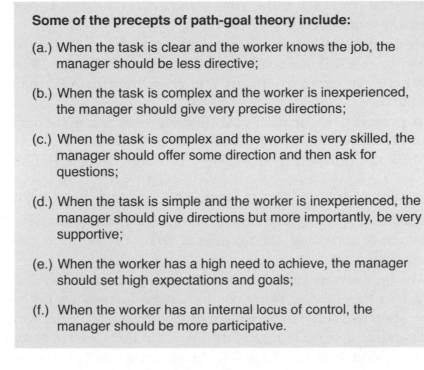

Some of the precepts of path-goal theory include:

(a.) When the task is clear and the worker knows the job, the manager should be less directive;

(b.) When the task is complex and the worker is inexperienced, the manager should give very precise directions;

(c.) When the task is complex and the worker is very skilled, the manager should offer some direction and then ask for questions;

(d.) When the task is simple and the worker is inexperienced, the manager should give directions but more importantly, be very supportive;

(e.) When the worker has a high need to achieve, the manager should set high expectations and goals;

(f.) When the worker has an internal locus of control, the manager should be more participative.

Chart 8: Path-Goal Theory based on House and Mitchell

Worker characteristics include (1) the worker's need for affiliation, (2) preferences for higher (or lower) structure, (3) the worker's locus of control, and (4) the self-perceived level of ability to accomplish the task.[15]

Task characteristics include (1) whether the work seems to be clear and ambiguous or whether it is task repetitive, (2) whether there is strong formal authority present, and (3) whether the group norms are clear. When the context of the situation is considered, the path-goal theory will suggest the optimal behavior style of managers for each specific situation.[16]

Directive behaviors include giving instructions, setting goals, and monitoring progress. For example, when the task is complex, and the workers are confused, managers give clear instructions about the task, how to perform the task and the timeline.

Supportive behaviors include involving, encouraging, and appreciating people. For example, when the job is unpleasant or even distressing, managers show care and concern for the emotional well-being of the workers and provide psychological support.

Participative behaviors include consulting and involving workers in decision-making processes. For example, when the worker has an *internal locus of control* (where they feel they make a direct impact on the world around them), managers consult more often.

Achievement-oriented behaviors are setting high goals for people and expecting them to reach those goals and meet those challenges. For example, when the workers are highly confident and competent people, managers set stretch goals for them.

From our perspective, the path-goal theory presents a more complete picture of the multitude of situational variables to be considered when managers are deciding how to approach their workers. By 1996, Robert House had provided twenty-six new hypotheses for his path-goal theory.[17] However, the theory draws criticism for being too complicated. As a result, it is rarely used for management training.[18] While the notion of adjusting the manager's behavior to fit the situation is appealing, the number of factors relevant to making such decisions seems almost infinite.

Most of the analysis we provided above to the "situational leadership" theory applies also to this theory. Many postindustrial factors are not considered by the theory, such as (1) the increasing cultural diversity of the workforce, (2) the technical versus adaptive nature of the work, (3) the speed of global change, (4) the hypercompetition in business, (5) the growing use of technology in the workplace, and so forth.

Today, the adaptive challenges facing most organizations are increasingly complex, requiring leaders and managers to be *assertive* about their ideas while also *cooperative* around the ideas of others (what we called Q4 behavior in chapter 5).

LEADER-MEMBER EXCHANGE

Leader-member exchange (LMX) theory looks at the interaction between "leaders and members."[19] Based on social research into group dynamics, it posits that people in positions of authority treat some people kindly as members of an *in-group*, while others are nearly forgotten as members of an *out-group*.

LMX was initially researched as a *descriptive* theory, which means the original intent was to describe the interactions of in-groups and out-groups.[20] It later developed into a *prescriptive* theory, with the intention to prescribe, or recommend, what managers should do.[21]

The theory submits that the interaction between managers and direct reports develops over three stages: (1) the *stranger* phase (where interaction is simply contractual), (2) the *acquaintance* stage (where interaction begins to go above pure self-interest), and (3) the *partner* phase (where interactions are reciprocal, based on trust and oriented toward the group's interests).

LMX proposes that the "high relationship exchanges" of the in-group produce more trust, commitment, and loyalty, while the "low relationship exchanges" of the out-group result in more distance and less trust.[22]

Because out-group members are perceived as less competent, less dedicated, less motivated, and less loyal (whether this is accurate or not), they receive less attention, fewer challenging assignments, and lower pay and benefits (chart 9).[23]

Research suggests that the performance of in-groups and out-groups can be the result of a *self-fulfilling prophecy*.[24] The greater attention, support, and confidence the in-group receives can be a direct cause of their higher performance, organizational commitment, and job satisfaction. Similarly, the lack of attention, support, and confidence displayed toward the out-group can be a causal factor in their lower performance, commitment, and satisfaction.[25]

From our perspective, the lessons of LMX can remind managers to be *individually considerate* of each person, as suggested by Bass.[26] This requires that managers take the time to become more aware of the special interests, distinct qualities, unique skills, and individual motivators of their people.

As Dale Carnegie pointed out in his 1936 classic book, *How to Win Friends and Influence People*, "You can make more friends in two months by becoming

LMX Theory

Outcomes of the in-group include:	Perceptions of the out-group is that they are:
1. better attitudes 2. more production 3. less turnover 4. better attendance 5. more promotions 6. more commitment to team goals	1. less competent 2. less dedicated 3. less motivated 4. less loyal 5. less reliable 6. less team-oriented
Therefore, they are given more attention, more challenging assignments, and better pay and benefits.	Therefore, they receive less attention, fewer challenging assignments, and lower pay and benefits.

Chart 9: LMX: In-groups vs. Out-groups
based on Graen and Uhl-Bien

interested in other people than you can in two years by trying to get other people interested in you."[27] When you take interest in others, they take an interest in you. You discover their varying sets of needs, concerns, and values. When you show that interest, you will also discover what motivates each member of your team.

Too often, people in authority decide who will be in their in-group or out-group based on their own personal needs and interests, and their biases about gender, age, ethnicity, or other factors. Members of the in-group often look *very much the same* as the person who put them there. This raises all sorts of ethical concerns. It can be demotivating for the workers who are assigned to the out-group for no fault of their own. The result is a self-fulfilling prophecy of less production, more turnover, worse attendance, bad attitudes, fewer promotions, and a reduced commitment to team goals from those who are thrown into the out-group.

The prescriptive lesson of LMX theory is this: Give everyone on your team every opportunity to join your in-group. Do everything you can to gain their trust. Listen to them. Consider their perspective. Treat everyone with the same level of dignity and respect.

CONCLUSION

Much can be salvaged from these traditional theories of the industrial era. They have common sense advice to people who are leading or managing from a position of authority. When relating to people who are direct reports, those in authority should consider such factors as (1) the readiness level of the worker, (2) the complexity of the task, and (3) other characteristics of the task and relationship.

However, we are concerned about what is *excluded* from these theories, such as (1) concern for adaptive change, (2) attention to cultural diversity, and (3) suggestions about how those in authority can create the necessary support and conditions for real leadership to take place. Managers can enhance leadership for the greater good when they (1) establish cultural norms that value participation and consultation, (2) work collaboratively to institute structures that allow shared decision-making at lower levels without requiring multiple levels of approval, and (3) launch strategies that reward initiative, innovation, and leadership with resources and support.

PART III
BEST PRACTICES IN LEADERSHIP

INTRODUCTION

We proceed to discuss four sets of leadership skills with this caveat: practicing a certain set of skills may improve your likelihood of success, but they do not *make* you a leader. Leadership is a collective process where influence is mutually shared. Leadership is greater than any one individual. No set of individual traits, behaviors, or skills can define the process of leadership or make you a leader.

Nevertheless, we think certain skills are critical to your success as a leader for the greater good, and we will present our case for them in these final four chapters. The emotional, dialogical, conflict, and strategic skills we discuss in this part of our book will begin with the *inward* journey of leadership, which means becoming a human being that is fully capable of engaging in the *outward* practice of leadership.[1]

One does not become fit by joining a fitness center. One does not become religious by joining a religion. Nor can you become a leader just by reading this leadership book. It takes training and practice to become more conscious of where you focus your attention, more mindful of your emotions, and more aware of the effect that your behavior is having on others. To succeed at leadership, certain skills must become daily habits.

As a collective activity, leadership takes place within daily interaction with others. It relies on healthy interactions between people. Any team or organization is a web of relationships. The first step in learning to practice the outward practice of leadership is to take the inward journey of becoming a better human being. Thus, leadership requires inside-out preparation. The work begins on the inside and moves toward the outside.

With this in mind, the order in which we will cover the skills presented in this section of our book will (1) begin with the inside work of emotional intelligence, (2) move toward the dialogical skills of communication, (3) deal with the inevitable situation where the team engages in conflict, and (4) present our case for developing strategies for leading change. In each chapter of this section, we hope to prepare our readers for the social context of leadership as a collective process involving colleagues, partners, and teammates.

A familiar adage comes to mind: "If you want to go fast, go alone. If you want to go far, go with a team." Many coaches, such as John Wooden, are fond of this quote.[2] Simply put, leadership is a collective activity that involves a team. We think that this explains why trust and collaboration are so important.[3] No collective activity can succeed without trust and collaboration, which can feed off each other in a virtuous cycle.

Synergy happens when the combined energy of a team achieves a result better than any single member could have come up with on their own. The best ideas can emerge from a team when they reach synergy. One idea bounces off another idea, and the team discovers a new collaborative idea. This should be the goal of every collaborative activity such as leadership.

Reaching synergy as a team becomes more critical in this world that has changed, is changing, and is becoming more complex. As organizations face more adaptive challenge, leaders welcome all viewpoints to the table. They level the playing field of decision-making and make sure everyone has a voice, especially those closest to the adaptive problem and those who have dissenting opinions.

In chapter 7, we present the emotional skills of leadership: self-awareness, self-control, social awareness, and social skills. Leading change invariably involves loss, which triggers emotional reactions. Emotional intelligence has become more critical as the workplace has become busier and the interaction more complex. Research shows that those who are not *self-aware* are rarely *socially aware.*[4] If you are not paying attention to what is going on inside your own heart and mind, you will rarely be successful in picking up on what is going on in the hearts and minds of those you are trying to lead.

In chapter 8, we explore dialogical skills—those needed for the dialogue that is necessary for the activity of leadership.[5] Leading change requires the ability to connect with others and understand their perspective in identifying and solving adaptive problems. Dialogue is the act of *thinking together* as a team.[6] Dialogue is also critical to the creation of trust, commitment, and loyalty. Given the global, cultural, and organizational diversity of today's workplace, and the complexity that comes from online communication and distance learning, dialogical communication skills have become even more critical.

In chapter 9, we describe three types of conflict—interest, factual, and normative—and explain how each type has a different solution path.[7] Leading change will invariably lead to conflict. We distinguish between *task conflict*, which can be healthy (in small to moderate amounts) to teams and organizations, versus *relationship conflict*, which is unhealthy in any amount.[8] At times, adaptive leadership requires that you introduce a healthy dose of task conflict into your leadership conversations, while preventing disagreements from escalating into relational conflict.

In chapter 10, we present the eight-step strategic planning process that Dan wrote with our colleague Fred Smith in *Strategic Planning: An Interactive Process for Leaders*. We distinguish between the role of leaders and managers, and the reciprocal role they have on each other. Managers create the formal structure for strategic planning while leaders create the open space that involves everyone in strategic conversations. Leaders shift the conversations toward adaptive instead of only technical issues. Together, leaders and managers insist on collaborative approaches to conflict, which is sure to erupt, and they facilitate the process of cocreating a vision for the future.[9]

CHAPTER 7

EMOTIONAL SKILLS

THE BRAIN AND THE MIND

What is the difference between the brain and the mind? Is the brain the seat and source of the mind or is it the other way around? Scientists and philosophers have pondered these questions for centuries. Modern research is changing the way science views the brain.[1] In the past, scientists believed that humans were born with all the brain neurons they were ever going to have. They also believed that most of human intelligence, personal disposition, and mental health was predetermined from birth. Those ideas are now considered relics in medical science.[2]

The human brain runs in patterns. Billions of neurons form pathways that are always changing and adapting to human sensations, choices, and experiences.[3] Science now teaches that the adult brain can generate new neurons instead of just rearranging the neurons it already has. This is called the *neuroplasticity* of the brain, its ability to reorganize itself, to change and grow.[4]

Leadership is a mindful practice that requires you to live fully in the present. The interactive nature of leadership demands that you *think* about what you really see—so that you can *see* what you really think. That requires engaging the prefrontal lobes of your brain and strengthening the neurological routes that connect to those lobes.

The conscious act of thinking about your thoughts, the willful act of changing the way you think, the intentional practice of being more aware of the patterns of the brain—all of this can change the neurological activities and structures of your brain.[5]

Where does this energy emerge from? Some say it is from the *mind*. The mind is that innate voice (some call it "self-talk," or "the movie in your head") or free will that allows humans to make conscious choices, to be aware of the habits of their thoughts and emotions, to practice restraint before acting.[6] It is what some call mind over matter, or more aptly, mind over brain. With mindful practice, the mind can have more control over the brain than vice versa. In fact, scientists now recognize the power of the mind to *transform the brain.*[7]

Jim Collins's seminal study, *Good to Great and the Social Sectors*, noted that the "gargantuan egos" of CEOs was a major factor in the demise or continued mediocrity of two-thirds of his comparison companies.[8] Matthias Birk points out that this lack of humility can bring out defensive tendencies at great cost to the interactions in a workplace. An inflated ego limits your ability to admit mistakes, receive critical feedback, and listen to your colleagues.[9]

Neuroscientific researchers are studying meditation as a means for people to experience "self-transcendence" and, in the process, to lessen their fixation on ego, enable them to see things more objectively, and facilitate deeper relationships. They are finding that taking a deep breath with focus can loosen the grip of your ego.[10] This is comparable to what Heifetz and Linsky would describe as "getting on the balcony" to see our inner actions, our interactions, and ourselves from afar.[11] However, the fast pace of human life, and the constant stimulation of the human world, make it difficult to employ the full power of mind over brain in daily life.

BRAIN FUNCTION

Let's look at four sections of the brain most critical to our conversation about leadership:

1. The *amygdala* is the deepest section of your primitive brain. It is designed for human protection and security: for fight, flight, or freeze. It has a back-alley neurological connection that allows you to act instantly and instinctively. It governs sensory motor and survival instincts. It can signal an instant hormonal reaction to a perceived threat.

2. The *limbic* system is your emotional center. Every physical sensation goes through the limbic system before it reaches the cognitive sections of your brain. This means that every thought has an emotion tied to it—even before you become consciously aware of the thought. It can trigger physiological reactions in blood flow to the heart and muscles.

3. The *neocortex* is the largest part of your brain. It is the seat of cognition, where thoughts and ideas are formed. Most humans do not come close to using the full capacity of this part of the brain. It processes data, governs language, and allows for critical thinking.

4. The *prefrontal cortex* is a key center for your neocortex. Not much brain activity reaches this area. It is where decisions and ideas can be processed consciously. It allows you to think about your thoughts, to be aware of your emotions, and to be conscious of your behaviors. This is where the mind can become a factor in brain function.[12]

There is a hierarchy here. The brain automatically defers to the amygdala when the person has not developed capacity in the neocortex. The amygdala operates only on the present moment. The rest of the limbic system can consider the past and the present to form emotions. It is only when the brain function reaches the neocortex, and especially the prefrontal lobes, that the brain fully considers the past, present, and future.[13]

When you are thinking about your past and present thoughts, and quietly scanning your past and present emotions, and silently reflecting on your own thoughts and considering what you might do in the future, you are engaging the left side of your prefrontal cortex (PFC). To the extent that you have engaged the heart in these reflections, you are also strengthening the neurological pathways between your head and your heart. In the process, you are becoming a more compassionate, considerate, and supportive human being—all of which can prepare you for the challenges of leadership.[14]

By engaging the parasympathetic nervous system in your body, you are softening your view of yourself and others. You are lowering your blood pressure, relaxing your muscles, and striking a healthy balance in your body. You are also literally strengthening the neurological connection between your head (specifically, the PFC) and your heart. In fact, some neuroscientists believe that the heart is another section of the brain.[15]

The activity of the heart can change the function of the brain—and vice versa. The human heart nurtures *empathy*, which is critical to leadership. Research shows that empathy, kindness, and concern for others can arise in the brain by nurturing the neurological connections between the physical heart and the left side of the prefrontal cortex.[16] However, empathy is counterintuitive for certain parts of the brain, which are wired to protect our self-interests.

When sensations are sent from any of the five senses to the brain, they must travel through the emotional (limbic) center of the brain before the sensation is processed by the neocortex (which includes the prefrontal cortex). This means that your thoughts and words are heavily influenced by emotional ties to every stimulus.[17] Unless you pause long enough to allow your brain activity to move all the way to the prefrontal cortex, and then to connect to the heart, you might give yourself a lot of selfish messages and thus, make a lot of selfish decisions. This is the design of the human brain. Its most primitive instincts are for self-preservation.

TRAINING THE MIND

Leaders must train their minds to think about what they want to think about.[18] With practice, you can refuse to wander into thoughts of your past or your future when you are supposed to be present to the person right in front of you.[19] You can improve your ability to focus your attention on listening when you are trying to practice adaptive leadership.

When you are holding a conversation with a coworker about an adaptive challenge, it is critical to practice the conscious, purposeful, and intentional practice of being attentive to what is happening right now, right in front of you. Neuroplasticity allows the brain to improve mindful functions because the brain is always open to new growth.[20] Neuroplasticity allows people to improve attention by practicing *mindfulness*. This can cause brain reorganization, where you reshape the habits of your brain through your daily practices—for better or worse.

A basketball player who is thinking about her postgame remarks in the fourth quarter might see the ball slip through her hands at a key moment, drastically changing what she is going to say in her postgame interview. One meeting gone awry can make it hard to focus on the next meeting. If you have someone come into your office and share some news that shakes you to your core, such as telling you they are going to quit, your emotional state can make it difficult to focus on the story of the next person who walks into your office.

Mindfulness involves thinking about your thoughts and redirecting your thoughts to consider another person's point of view or to focus on something more positive.[21] Mindfulness helps you to capture the moment, to be aware of your sensations and conscious of your feelings. It reminds you to awaken mindfully, walk mindfully, meditate mindfully, pause mindfully, and wait mindfully. When leading others, it helps you to listen intently to what the other person is saying, hearing that person as if for the first time, being fully present to them, letting their words soak in and intuiting their emotions with gentleness and care. Human beings pay attention to what they are *sensitive* to.

A BORING MEETING

Let's say you are in a meeting and you are watching the meeting degrade into one boring report after another. Instead of focusing on what is going wrong, you can focus on what you are going to do next. Spend your mental energy on positive solutions for the things that are going wrong instead of obsessing over the problem. Develop a positive mindset. Ask, What would it take to get this meeting back on track? After the meeting, reflect on the interaction. Talk to the people running the meeting and make positive suggestions for change. Come to the next meeting ready to share ideas about how your meetings can be more productive.

When you are in a meeting, mindfulness cultivates a conscious awareness of your thoughts, emotions, and sensations. Your mind interprets what the brain is sensing. You can interrupt any negative biases in your thinking. You can look at everything being said and done with greater openness and curiosity. You can develop new habits of being receptive to new viewpoints. You can engage the heart and become kinder toward others, forgiving instead of judging, focusing on the positive and the beautiful, with intent and purpose.

The amygdala tends toward the negative.[22] Its job is to defend and protect. It is designed to look for any attack and quickly alert you to it. To overcome its negativity, it takes a lot of positive energy and attention. Focus on what is going well. Think about the values and interests of others. Connect to your common set of values and interests. Reflect on your purpose. Trust your prefrontal cortex to guide you through this process.[23]

EMOTIONAL INTELLIGENCE

Employers are seeking well-rounded candidates who can work well with others, put their problem-solving skills to use, and face challenging situations with dignity and grace. Many employers complain that such employees are few and far between.

Emotional intelligence has been described by Daniel Goleman and subsequent research as a more accurate predictor of leadership success than technical or cognitive skills.[24] In fact, your *emotional quotient* (EQ) is a better predictor of success in life and leadership than your intelligence quotient (IQ). A high EQ unleashes your full IQ potential. A low EQ limits your potential because fear, anger, worry, prejudice, jealousy, anxiety, and ignorance will limit your performance.

IQ is described by Goleman as a "threshold competence."[25] It gets you in the door for an interview, and possibly gets you hired. EQ is a "distinguishing competence" that will set you apart as a top performer after you are hired. We suggest these four areas (chart 10) add up to emotional intelligence:[26]

1. Self-awareness: Ability to recognize your own emotions
2. Self-control: Ability to regulate your own behaviors
3. Social awareness: Ability to identify with the emotions of others
4. Social skills: Ability to handle the emotions for others

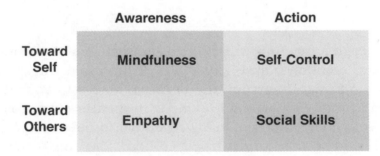

Chart 10: Four Parts of Emotional Intelligence
based on Daniel Goleman

SELF-AWARENESS (MINDFULNESS)

Self-awareness begins when you pause long enough to think about your emotions and how they are impacting your thoughts, intentions, and behaviors. This is a special human talent that is part of what scientists call *proprioception*, or "self-perception,"[27] which includes the ability to think about your thoughts, reflect on your emotions, consider your intentions, and evaluate your behaviors.

Self-awareness begins in what Victor Frankl describes as a magical moment "between stimulus and response."[28] It is that moment between sensation and action, between the trigger event and your reaction to it. It is in that moment of reflection, when you stop long enough to open your mind, your heart, and your will—so you can think, feel, and choose differently.

That slight pause is a *moment of grace*, a moment in time that presents itself when you become fully awake to the present moment. Self-awareness helps you sense a change in emotions and understand what that change is doing to your physical energy and how it is affecting your thoughts and actions.

BACK TO THAT BORING MEETING

Let's say you are still sitting in a boring meeting. The moment you identify your emotion as *boredom*, you become self-aware. Boredom can have an impact on your thoughts, emotions, intentions, and behaviors. Perhaps your thoughts have strayed from the content of the meeting. Perhaps you are looking at your phone. Others might notice you are bored before you do. When you project boredom, you send a message to the person speaking that you are no longer interested in them or what they are saying. It can be a sign of disrespect.

Most of the time, people are oblivious to the impact that their emotions are having on their behavior—and that of others. Changing your behavior in a meeting begins with self-awareness. Especially when you are practicing leadership, your emotional reactions can be under a microscope. The emotions of the rest of the team can be dependent upon the emotions of the leader. They are looking for cues as to how they should react.[29]

Somewhere between the moment of a stimulus and the moment of response is an *opportunity for leadership*. In that moment of grace, you can be mindful. You can think about your thoughts, your plans, your intentions, and your reactions in real time. Research by Goleman shows that without self-awareness, it is unlikely that you will practice well the other three areas of emotional intelligence: self-control, social awareness, or social skills.[30]

Travis Bradberry and Jean Greaves suggest some ways to improve on self-awareness:[31]

- Know what things push your emotional buttons.
- Recognize when you are in a bad mood.
- Ask yourself, "Why am I feeling this way?"
- Notice what grabs your attention in music, art, theatre, movies.
- Seek feedback from trusted colleagues.

SELF-CONTROL

If self-awareness presents you with the dashboard to recognize your emotions, *self-control* is the ability to use that information to guide your behavior. When you become aware, you are more likely to practice self-control.[32] However, sometimes people just don't care enough. Perhaps they don't want to change their behavior. They might figure they can get what they want by acting angry, bored, frustrated, or upset.

Let's say you are running a meeting and you are starting to lose your patience. You can feel the anger building up inside your limbic system, which is shooting chemical reactions through your blood stream. You could lash out angrily, and perhaps that would shock people and bully them, so you get what you want—temporarily. However, the results will be fleeting. People living in a dictatorship will comply only if they have no other choice.

Anger can blind people to the perspective of others. The signal for anger immediately sends adrenaline to your fists. This probably explains why people want to hit something (or someone) when they get angry. Anger without self-awareness can spell certain doom for your meetings. You are more likely to say things you will regret later.[33]

The signal for fear sends adrenaline to your feet. It makes you want to run away. When the person in authority in a group explodes with anger, most people in the room become afraid. They want to run. They are unlikely to speak up. If their perspective on an adaptive challenge is important, you will be missing that piece of information.

Anger can damage your ability to feel empathy. Fear can impair your ability to take risks, even prudent ones. Worry can drain you of the energy you need for further dialogue. Negative emotions that are not managed well can destroy you—and if you are leading, they can bring down those around you.[34]

When under the influence of negative emotions, it is important to buy time. Psychologists call this *cognitive reappraisal*, where you actively try to reframe your initial perception to regulate your emotions under duress.[35] You can pause, drink a sip of water, ask a question of clarification, try not to spill your guts right away while you allow time for your prefrontal lobes to reappraise, or reframe, the events around you. Taking a long exhale with your next breath can help you to activate your parasympathetic nervous system. This literally signals the release of chemicals that can help you begin to relax and think more clearly.

Emotionally intelligent leaders use their self-awareness to reflect on their thoughts and emotions, and to change their self-talk, so they can improve their interactions with others.[36] They gain a more objective view of reality. They reshape their behaviors. They choose to go a different route. Acting without self-awareness is like driving a car without a gauge that measures your engine temperature. Acting without self-control is like driving your car after the gauge shows that the engine is boiling over. It can destroy the engine. In a meeting, overreacting with anger, fear, or frustration can destroy the trust you have carefully built into your leadership relationship.

Reflection on your behavior can break the vicious cycle of emotional outbursts and mindful regrets. Reflection occurs in the prefrontal cortex (PFC). It allows for a more refined, balanced, and mindful approach. The PFC can serve as the place where a reappraisal of the situation can take place. It is the place where mindful planning and organizing of fresh ideas can occur—if you can guide your thoughts through reflection.

Self-monitoring is the ability to reflect on your cycle of behavior on a regular basis. Ask yourself, *How aware was I of the emotions I experienced in that last meeting? How well did I manage those emotions? What could I do differently the next time my coworker acts like that in a meeting?* Reflection on these questions is using your PFC to think about your thoughts and consider your options.

Bradberry and Greaves suggest these ways to improve on self-control:[37]

- Pay conscious attention to your breath.
- Pause to take a sip of water or coffee before you speak in a meeting.
- List your emotions versus your reasons for a certain decision.
- Sleep on major decisions.
- Smile and laugh more often—it can trick the brain into positivity.
- Focus on self-talk—the messages the mind sends to the brain.

SOCIAL AWARENESS (EMPATHY)

Social awareness is the ability to recognize the emotions of others.[38] It allows you to understand how your interactions are affecting the emotions in the room. This requires great empathy—which is made more difficult when you are experiencing emotional trauma of your own, such as when you are experiencing conflict with a colleague.

Let's say you are in a meeting. It is getting very heated. Your limbic system is sending adrenaline through your veins. Empathy is the ability to get outside of your own emotional reactions, to think outside your amygdala (your own selfish ego), and to understand what others are experiencing emotionally in that moment. It is the ability to think and feel with your heart, and to frame the emotional reactions of others in a positive, nonjudgmental way.

Empathy is a choice. When the amygdala is screaming for attention, trying to tell you, "So and so is attacking you," or "You don't have to take that kind of treatment from anyone," empathy can enter in—if you engage the heart. Empathy calls you to pay attention to the needs and interests of others. When you are upset yourself, empathy is very counterintuitive.[39]

Sympathy is more of an instinctive response. It means to "feel sorry" for someone. You hear about someone who just lost a spouse, or you see a homeless mother and child on the street, and you automatically feel sympathy. That is not empathy. Empathy demands that you do something about the predicament of others.[40]

The plasticity of the brain allows for retraining to become more empathetic, more positive, and more aware of what is going on around us. You can train yourself to become more empathetic by developing stronger neurological connections to your heart.[41] To be empathetic is to choose the heart over the amygdala. It requires mindful attention to listen to the heart center during a conversation. First, you must turn off the loud voice of the amygdala. Second, you must purposely consider the other person's perspective. When you involve the heart in decision-making, you are choosing trust over fear, wisdom over control, humility over pride, and altruism over selfishness.

Some ways to improve on social awareness are the following:[42]

- Study the cultural norms of body language.
- Jot down notes after a meeting, so you can pay more attention during the meeting.
- Ask the right question to the right person at the right time.
- Reflect on what other people are going through.
- Concentrate on letting the other person finish before you speak.
- Go people watching to study how they interact with each other.

SOCIAL SKILLS

Imagine you are in a meeting. Things are getting emotional. To facilitate the interaction of your team during such moments, you need to (1) be attentive to your own emotions, (2) guide your behaviors despite your own emotions, (3) pick up on the emotional cues of others, and (4) act with empathy toward others in the room. These are the four parts of emotional intelligence (EI).[43]

Your ability to empathize is strongly related to your emotional security. When you are enduring an amygdala hijack, it becomes almost impossible to think about others.[44] You must first calm your own rage, control your own fears, or console your own frustrations. Only then can you think straight.

Emotions are contagious. Seeing a person cry can bring on your own tears. Hearing others laugh can make you laugh until you cry. The emotions of a leader have a special effect on the whole team. When the leader can create an atmosphere of emotional security, the people are more likely to act with empathy.[45]

The first step in guiding the interaction of a team during an emotional episode is to demonstrate empathy. When a leader shows empathy, it has a multiplying effect on the rest of the team. People are more likely to empathize, to trust each other, to collaborate with each other, to work as a team, to help each other out, and to take the initiative on new projects.[46]

Acting with empathy changes the wiring inside your brain. It allows your sense of empathy to trump your sense of fear. Emotional distraught prevents human beings from empathizing with others. When you demonstrate concern for another person, you *change the neural activity in your own brain.*[47] You strengthen the neurological connections between your head and your heart—the path to empathy.

People live with regrets for *yesterday* and worries about *tomorrow.* Yesterday and tomorrow can prevent you from living today—in the *present* moment. They inhibit your ability to be present to the present. In fact, the two biggest obstacles to living fully in the present moment are (1) the past and (2) the future. To act with all four steps of EI, you must be fully awake to the present moment.

Some ways to improve on people skills are the following:[48]

- Call people by name—focus on learning names.
- Study and discuss the cultural norms of your organization.
- Listen with intention and purpose.
- Summarize what the other person is saying.
- When someone else is having an amygdala hijack, name the emotion.
- Encourage feedback about how you are doing.

CONCLUSION

The human heart is where people can *connect* with each other. Neuroscientists teach that the key to happy, healthy, and fulfilling lives is forming the connections between the heart and the brain.[49] When people stop to consider the point of view of another person, they are using that same neurological pathway between the head and the heart. Those pathways must be strengthened if you are going to practice leadership for the greater good.

The research on emotional intelligence provides practical insights to improve leadership. Given the interactive nature of leading adaptive change, and the busy environment of workplaces today, the need has grown for (1) self-awareness, (2) self-control, (3) social awareness, and (4) social skills. They are critical to practicing the dialogical, conflict, and strategic skills we describe in the next three chapters.

CHAPTER 8

DIALOGICAL SKILLS

TRUST AND COLLABORATION

Given the new reality of the postindustrial era, with the growing diversity of the workplace, increasing complexity of the work, rising demands of globalization, and hypercompetitive environment of our rapidly changing business world, every organization is experiencing an increase in adaptive challenges (chapter 1). Because of this, and the excessive reliance on technology for communication, it has become ever more critical for leaders to improve the dialogical skills that can engage others to identify adaptive problems, understand various perspectives, and explore solutions.

Dialogue is a way of thinking, reflecting, and conversing together so that a team can find answers that no individual could have imagined by themselves.[1] Generally, when the collective wisdom of the group can be harnessed and directed toward an adaptive problem, the insight is greater than any individual could muster. Dialogue can create a deeper sense of meaning and understanding about the nature of a problem and what needs to be done. It can also build healthy, trusting relationships that nurture leadership to emerge from within.

Trust is the foundation of the dialogical skills we will discuss in this chapter. Trust grows from dialogue. Some trust is necessary *before* dialogue and the level of it increases *after* dialogue. Trust builds commitment to the team while commitment to the team builds trust. Trust increases the likelihood of success while success builds trust. Building trust is so integral to leadership that we begin our discussion of leadership skills by exploring the dialogical skills that build trust.

Leadership cannot exist without trust.[2] Trust is the essence of social capital, which is the sum total of social relationships in a workplace.[3] Trust is critical to all working relationships. According to Patrick Lencioni, "Trust lies at the heart of a functioning, cohesive team. Without it, teamwork is all but impossible."[4] Without trust, teams cannot address conflict, build commitment, hold each other accountable, or achieve great results.[5] Trust is both the *glue* that holds everything together on a team and the *grease* that makes it all work.

Trust and collaboration have a reciprocal relationship, which means they propel each other. They go hand in hand. The more people trust, the more they can collaborate. The more they collaborate, the more they can trust. Trust and collaboration are either working through a *vicious cycle*, where both are declining in synch with each other, or a *virtuous cycle*, where they are flourishing together.

Trust is conditional. Trust depends on the honesty, loyalty, and respect of both parties. You can develop trust yourself by being *trustworthy* (which means you are "worthy of trust"), but you cannot develop trust simply by trusting others.[6] Trust is earned through integrity. When you act with *integrity*, you "integrate" your values and your behaviors. You act on your values. You practice what you preach. You do what you say. You build trust.

You cannot always rely on others to act in a trustworthy manner. It is not totally within your control. However, you can model honest behavior and that encourages others to be honest. You can schedule time for people to get to know each other and that helps to build a circle of trust within your team.[7] Spending time on relationships can build rapport and fuel the positive connection between trust and collaboration.

A lot has been said about the need for "soft skills" in today's workplace. We prefer the term "complex people skills," as our colleague Randy Richards calls it, instead of "soft skills," but the point is that leadership requires the ability to communicate, resolve conflicts, build teams, make decisions, plan strategically, and act with flexibility. All these aspects of leadership involve dialogical skills.

The problem is that most organizations hire only for technical skills, not people skills, even when it is easier to teach and improve technical skills than it is to teach and improve people skills.[8] When people who are hired for technical skills are promoted into middle and upper levels of authority, the need for people skills grows further. Many of our own students are professionals who were promoted into positions of authority because of their technical skills. They enroll in our leadership classes to develop people skills.

If technical skills are the "hard skills," perhaps people skills should be regarded as the "harder skills." It seems harder to size up people than numbers, harder to reconcile relationships than bank statements, and harder to balance priorities than financial statements. Organizations need more emphasis on teaching, training, and enhancing people skills. With people skills, leaders can facilitate the type of dialogue that is so critical to building trust and solving adaptive challenges.

ASKING INSTEAD OF TELLING

Edgar Schein says we live in a "culture of do and tell."[9] Let's consider how the culture of our organizations might change if we took a different approach. What might happen if we led by *asking* instead of *telling*? How could asking questions, instead of telling answers, encourage more leadership to emerge?

A STORY OF ASKING VS. TELLING

Imagine a man approaches his boss on a Friday and tells him, "I've got to take off work on Monday." Imagine the boss responds by telling him, "There is no way you can get off on Monday. I've got three people taking that day off already." The worker curses at his boss, and the boss curses back. The worker proceeds down the hall and files a complaint with his union, stating that (a) his boss would not let him take Monday off, even though his wife was having major surgery that day, and (b) he swore at him. Technically, the worker was right on both counts.

Imagine how differently this story would go if either or both parties had used asking instead of telling. Let's suggest that the worker asks, "John, is there any way I can have off on Monday?" John replies, "Hey, Tom, what is happening on Monday?" (Note that both parties in this version of the conversation start with a question, not a statement.) Tom replies, "Well, I just found out my wife is having major surgery on Monday and I need to be with her." John replies, "Well, I've already got three people taking off on Monday, but hey, Tom, I'll cover your shift for you myself."

The simple act of *asking instead of telling* can change the dynamics of stories like this one.[10] The worker gets the day off to be with his wife during her surgery. The boss is not subjected to a union grievance.

When you are in a position of authority, the tendency is to be more assertive in telling and less cooperative in listening.[11] That is human nature, especially in a culture of do and tell. Our culture rewards us for what we do and what we tell. The idea of asking and listening is a foreign concept for many bosses. However, if you want to address adaptive challenges, where the answers tend to be elusive, it is much wiser to ask and to listen.

LEADING WITH QUESTIONS

Leading with questions is both an art and a science. The *art* includes (1) being truly humble about your own shortcomings and curious about the views of others;[12] (2) shedding your own selfish notions that you must be the one with the right answer or the best solution;[13] (3) placing yourself humbly at the service of your team; and (4) presenting an attitude of *assertive vulnerability*, which is not about weakness but accessibility, conveying that you are open to change and willing to admit limitations and mistakes.[14]

The *science* is using the right prompts: (1) open-ended questions that invite the other person to take the conversation in their own direction; (2) encouraging responses that indicate interest and attention; (3) summaries that instill confidence that you are listening; and (4) clarifying questions that help you understand.[15]

Michael Marquardt suggests that asking (instead of telling) is one way to build *social capital*, which equates to higher levels of trust, commitment, and cohesion.[16] Asking questions can nurture a culture where everyone is on a search for truth. In most organizations, some people have perspectives and suggestions that are hidden from view. Many of them are just waiting to be asked, or to find someone in authority who has an open mind to listen.

The simple act of asking can encourage those who have something to contribute but have never shared their ideas. Until those in authority create a safe place to speak out, too many people will just keep waiting to be asked. They will comply with orders but hesitate to volunteer their time, their talent, or their ideas beyond minimal expectations.[17]

To lead with questions requires (a) the *wisdom* to know that you don't know everything, (b) the *humility* to admit that to others, and (c) the *courage* to act accordingly. Edgar Schein's humble inquiry is one way to lead with questions.

HUMBLE INQUIRY

Humble inquiry (HI) is a systematic way to ask questions for which you don't already know the answers.[18] The humble inquirer asks questions with (1) humility, (2) empathy, and (3) genuine curiosity (chart 11). Humble inquiry

Humble Inquiry

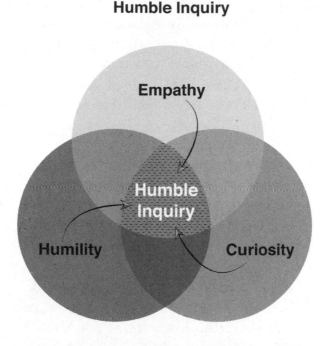

Chart 11: Humble Inquiry
based on Edgar Schein

offers a way to hold critical conversations about issues that matter. The key is to see the other person as your teacher and to see yourself as the learner.

The word *humility* comes from the Latin word *humus*, which means "from the earth." It shares the same origin as the word *human*. To be humble is to be human. It means to be down to earth, to be grounded in the reality of your strengths and your weaknesses, recognizing that you are a human being who always has something to learn.[19]

To be *humble* means to get your hands *dirty*, to dig into the thoughts and ideas of others instead of digging into your own positional thinking. Humility teaches that the more you know, the more you realize you don't know. Faults, weaknesses, and mistakes show that you are *human*, which is the basis of humility.

Admitting weakness becomes a sign of strength. The strength of humility lies in recognizing your weakness, so you no longer need to hide that weakness. Admitting you cannot do everything frees you up to find other members of the team to cover for that weakness. Admitting you don't know everything frees you up to inquire of others what you do not know.

Humble inquiry is a way to find out what others know, instead of telling others what you know. It is a way to find out what others see, instead of telling

---

others what you see. The sheer act of asking instead of telling implies that you are eager to know and see what they know and see, and to find what they have found.

Humble inquiry is especially powerful when practiced by those in authority. It levels the playing field because in most cases, those in authority are expected to tell more and ask less, while their direct reports are expected to ask more and to tell less.

Increasingly, in this complex and fast-moving world, managers and leaders need to find out what others think. They need the input of others to identify problems, explore solutions, and make decisions. Humble inquiry opens the other person to share things that you don't know. It is searching for the best possible solution rather than convincing people that you are right.

Humility implies being open to the possibility that you are wrong. *Inquiry* means asking questions to find out what the other person is thinking. Advocacy is the opposite of inquiry.[20] It means convincing others that you are right. The questions you ask can easily slip into advocacy if you ask *leading* or *loaded* questions, such as, "You don't think we should do that, do you?"[21] That is a statement disguised as a question. It is neither humble nor inquiring.

Daniel Coyle says that by demonstrating *vulnerability*, a person in authority can make it safe for others to speak out without fear of reprisal.[22] He suggests saying things like, "This is just my two cents worth," or "Of course, I could be wrong here," or "Please feel free to speak up." Questions like, "What am I missing?" and "What do you really think?" can encourage people to speak up. After they share their views, be overly generous with the thank yous. If you criticize their views, it may be the last time they speak up. When those in authority make themselves vulnerable, those without authority are more likely to say what they really think.

BEING VULNERABLE

Let's say that a surgeon is about to operate on the wrong patient, or the wrong shoulder. If no one in the operating room is willing to speak out, the result could be disastrous. The person in authority who demonstrates vulnerability—by openly admitting that he is capable of making mistakes—will build confidence in others to know that they can speak out, especially when he is about to make a mistake.

R. D. Laing suggests that many people in authority face the quandary of needing input from others but being afraid to admit it. He describes their thinking in this way: "I feel you know what I'm supposed to know, but you can't tell me what it is, because you don't know that I don't know what it is."[23] Instead of asking, their thinking goes this way: "There is something I don't know that I am supposed to know. I don't know what it is I don't know, and I feel I look stupid if I seem to not know what it is that I don't know. Therefore, I pretend I know it."[24]

Asking thought-provoking, open-ended, honest questions is the first step in humble inquiry. Then you listen. Just listen. Once you have listened, with full concentration on what is being said (instead of rehearsing what you are going to say or ask next), you summarize what you have heard, and pause to see if you got it right. The next question, if it is needed, should emerge out of the conversation (not rehearsed in advance). Lock into what the other person is saying, and the next question will arise out of what they have said. Let your curiosity be your guide. Resist the temptation to tell the other person what you think (that comes later). Ask questions that will help you gain their full perspective without tainting their idea with yours.

OPEN QUESTIONS

The best way to open a humble conversation is with an open-ended question. Examples of *open-ended* questions are the following: "What are you working on?" "How are you doing on the project?" "Tell me about X." They encourage others to be honest and direct as they express *what*, describe *how*, or explain *why*. Open questions indicate that you are truly open to what the other person wants to say. A closed question limits the other person to only what you are interested in hearing.

Once you ask an open question, your job is to demonstrate that you are following their story. Your next question should stay *within their story*, instead of changing the subject. Your goal is to allow them to express their thoughts, feelings, and ideas, and to probe further for meaning, not to project your thoughts, feelings, or ideas onto them. By summarizing their ideas, you not only show interest, you can clarify meaning. Using an inquisitive tone to your summary allows the other person to correct your summary if necessary.

Try not to hijack their story by telling your story, making your suggestions, changing the subject, or asking leading, loaded, or closed questions that suggest a solution or steer the person toward what you think, or what you think the other person should think, do, or say. You will get your chance to express your views later, after you hear their full story.

Inadvertently or not, some of the questions you ask might shift the focus to *your* point of interest or steer the conversation in *your* direction. Leading questions are statements about your ideas put in the form of a question, such as "You like John's idea, don't you?" or "You're with me on this one, right?" These are questions that fit your narrative or swing the attention of the conversation toward your ideas and interests. This is not humble inquiry. When you ask an open question, try to refrain from judging how it fits into your narrative, until you have heard the entire story.

Closed questions are *either-or* questions. They search for a definitive response, such as yes or no. They seek a specific answer to a specific situation. Generally, they are a way to control the conversation instead of providing the opportunity for the other person to take the initiative. Some are helpful to clarify a situation, such as "When is our next meeting?" or "What is on the agenda?" However, most closed questions steer the conversation in the direction of the person asking the questions. Open questions allow the other person to take the conversation in the direction they want it to go and then express what is on their mind.

OPEN VS. CLOSED QUESTIONS

Let's say your child returns home from school and you ask, "How was your day?" That is an open question that allows the child to take the conversation in any direction. On the other hand, if you ask, "How was school...did you get an *A* on your test?" that limits the response to one specific part of the day. Note how that question starts with an open question, but quickly follows with a closed question. This is a common mistake. The quick, follow-up, closed question has a way of retracting an effective, open question and pointing directly to the part of the story you want to hear.

Closed questions can be useful when you need to clarify what the other person is saying, such as, "Did you say X is the problem?" or "When did you first see the problem develop?" Generally, closed questions are more suitable to addressing a technical problem, whereas open questions are more applicable to an adaptive challenge. Open questions do not push our preconceived impressions or beliefs. When you come into a meeting by delivering a charismatic speech, or begin the conversation by forcefully stating your opinion, you cannot expect others to be open to sharing their thoughts, feelings, and ideas so readily.

AN ACCUSATORY QUESTION

Let's say that someone makes a mistake, and the boss says, "How could you possibly think that this was the best way to handle the situation?" Technically, this is a question. But the answer is assumed in the question. It is an *accusatory* question, one that expects the other person to admit that they were wrong and should have handled something differently. The person being asked is probably just going to say they are sorry or do whatever they can to get out of trouble. This type of question is neither humble nor inquiring.

Consider if the person asks an open question like, "Why did you decide to handle the situation in that manner?" Just a slight change to the previous question. But this invites a conversation about the mistake that was made. Both people are more likely to learn something with this approach. It presents both sides with the opportunity to teach and to learn what different options may have been better. Either way, the relationship might grow between the two because the leader showed respect for that person, and that person will be more likely to be open to change and more willing to communicate with the leader in the future.

Just as important as what you include in your humble inquiry toolbox is what you exclude: your thoughts, judgments, and opinions (at least until you have fully listened to the other person and summarized their views). The human tendency is to respond quickly with your views, or to ask questions that suggest solutions and test whether the other person agrees with you, such as "Have you tried X?" Instead, in humble inquiry, your job is to listen and to understand, not to state your ideas or to test whether the other person agrees with your ideas.

We find that if you (1) humbly ask questions, (2) show interest in the other's point of view, (3) summarize what they are saying, and (4) show respect and appreciation for their perspective (without necessarily agreeing with it), that increases the *receptivity* of the other person or people in a conversation. Eventually, they will say, "You understand what I think about this....What do you think we should do?" At that point, they are much more receptive to your ideas and much more likely to listen and understand your viewpoint as well.

Leading with questions creates a welcoming atmosphere of openness and respect. When you are asking instead of telling, especially when you are in a position of authority, it can change the culture of your organization. It encourages other people to step up and lead.

Humility and vulnerability are contagious. Once you begin to act with humility, others will too. Eventually, you will find that people will lose track of things like who gets the credit and who gets the blame. You can act like a team on a mission.

DEFLECTION

To *deflect* is another useful communication tool for leadership. When someone asks a good question, it is tempting to answer it right away. To *deflect* is to turn the question back to the group. This is especially helpful when the power distance is high between you and the rest of the group. When the authority figure speaks first, it ends the conversation for some people. Instead, you might say, "That's a great question. What do others think?"

ASK, THEN LISTEN

Once you ask the right questions, you listen. As Schein explains,[25]

1. Listen to the words and the emotions behind the words.
2. Demonstrate that you understand by summarizing and reflecting.
3. Show that you care by empathizing.

To listen is to *tune into* someone else.[26] It helps you to connect with others. It builds relationships. It shows that you care. It opens the door for an honest exchange. It raises the *receptivity* of the other person to listen to what you want to say. As the adage goes, People don't *care* how much you know...until they *know* how much you care.

Listening is an investment that takes time and patience. Given the rapid pace and perpetual nature of change in the world today, most people tend to speed everything up, including conversations. They do not allow enough time for the single-minded listening that ensures open, honest, and effective communication. The irony is that they waste time when they do not get the message right the first time and need to go back to fix their mistakes.

Listening is opening yourself up to being influenced by others. It is making yourself vulnerable to the possibility that you may be wrong. Listening can allow the other person to lead. By showing an interest in others, you can create the conditions by which new leaders emerge. Listening to critical or constructive feedback, without becoming defensive or taking it personally, is a powerful tool for developing the leadership potential of others.

Humble inquiry affirms the other person. It helps the other person clarify what he or she thinks. It encourages others to speak up and present their viewpoints. It helps to build a culture of "ask and listen" instead of "do and tell." Generally, when someone asks you a question, and the issue is *adaptive* in nature, your first instinct should be to ask, "What do you think?"

DIALOGUE

Dialogue is a conversation suitable to what Rost describes as leaders and followers doing leadership together. Dialogue is a conversation in which people *think together*.[27] Dialogue nurtures new insights. It challenges the process.[28] It questions *tacit assumptions*, meaning the things taken for granted. Dialogue confronts the attitude that says, "We tried that before and it doesn't work," or "That's just how we do things around here."

A dialogue is not the same as concurrent monologues.[29] To think together, focus your full attention on what the other person is saying instead of rehearsing what you will say in response. Postpone your preconceived notions of what the other person is going to say. Create the mental space for leadership to take place. Live fully in the present moment, with full attention on what the other person is saying.[30]

Dialogue is a *conversation with a center*, not sides.[31] When the thoughts and emotions of a team are in synch with each other, the people reach a new center, with higher levels of reciprocal sharing. One idea turns into another idea and together they create a harmonious idea that neither party could have developed on its own. No one takes credit for the idea because it was the result of teamwork.

Dialogue harnesses the collective energy of the team. It generates synergistic thinking. It inspires new and collaborative solutions. Dialogue is a great fit for adaptive solutions because it is precisely the type of conversation that can unpack the complexities of today's workplace.

Dialogue improves relationships. Thinking, reflecting, and acting together strengthens the bonds of those involved in dialogue. The improved relationships further improve the next dialogue. We encounter a *virtuous* cycle where the more you dialogue, the better your relationships, and…the better your relationships, the better your next dialogue.

Dialogue is *countercultural* to an individualist culture, where people are more accustomed to thinking and acting alone. The Greek word for "dialogue" means to gather in search of new meaning. The Greeks understood that new meaning could only be discovered *collectively*. Dialogue is a conversation by people in relationship who are committed to search for a deeper sense of meaning.

Dialogue is also *reciprocal*. The genuine climate of give-and-take is a mutual exchange that benefits each person. Dialogue fits the Rost definition of leadership because it is a multidirectional street. The conversation can include top-down, bottom-up, peer-to-peer, inside-out, and outside-in.

Dialogue is *dialectic*. It brings divergent ideas and opinions together in a search for shared meaning. It is not about winners and losers—as in a debate. Each person (or each side) commits to reach a higher level of understanding. This can happen whenever people think, speak, and reason through a problem together.

In a debate, each side pushes its own agenda while resisting what others are saying. To *debate* literally means to "beat down." The goal in a debate is to "convince," which literally means to win. A debate assumes a zero-sum game: one side wins while the other side loses. There is no win/win. Dialogue creates opportunities for both sides winning, which is the essence of collaboration (chapter 9).

Ironically, most people wish the combatants on the *other* side of a debate would pay more attention to their side. Each party sees the other as pushing their own point of view. The paradox here is that in most cases, both parties seem unaware that they are doing precisely the same thing. They are treating others the opposite way that they want to be treated. This is the *golden rule in reverse*: doing unto others what you don't want the other to do to you.

Debate is a highly controlled exchange with both parties making their points, warding off attacks, competing for air time, attributing the worst of motives to the other side, advocating their own positions, and beating the other side down to reach a conclusion that is usually unsatisfactory to both parties.

A dialogue can easily turn into a debate unless the leader is teaching and modeling the dialogical skills we are suggesting here. This is particularly true for online communication or phone conversations, where it is more difficult to be fully present to each other. It is all too natural for people to interrupt each other with knee-jerk reactions or to shoot off an angry email. Emotional reactions are much harder to gauge when we are not in face-to-face dialogue.

FOUR PRACTICES FOR HEALTHY DIALOGUE

Isaacs shares four practices that are the building blocks for dialogue: (1) listening, (2) respecting, (3) suspending, and (4) voicing.[32]

1. *Listening* is more than just hearing words. It is embracing and accepting what the other person is saying, intuiting the feelings behind the words, and reflecting on what is being expressed.
2. *Respecting* means literally to "look again." When you respect someone, you look again and see what you missed. You recognize the dignity of the other person as a distinct human being.
3. *Suspending* is withholding your judgment or holding back on forming a premature opinion. When you suspend your opinion, you demonstrate that you are still open to consider all options. When you form your opinion too soon—and especially when you share it with everyone else—you demonstrate that you have closed your mind. The temptation is to defend that opinion when others present a different view.
4. *Voicing* is speaking your voice, sharing what you think, feel, and believe. At some point in the conversation, you will need to be assertive and present your views. It is important to be assertive and cooperative at the same time (Q4). It is important to restrain yourself from speaking your voice too soon. Generally, the other

person is going to be more receptive to your thoughts and ideas after you have listened, understood, and appreciated their contrary viewpoint.

In a dialogue, everyone takes turns. When one person finishes their response, everyone else has a choice: (a) to continue listening, or (b) to assert their own thoughts, opinions, and positions. While you are listening, respecting, and suspending, it is hard to stay focused on what others are saying without *rehearsing* what you want to voice. Mindfulness becomes so important (chapter 7).

In a dialogue, you *deliberate*, which means to "weigh out," that is, to decide what you weigh as deeming your attention and what is not worth your attention. You deliberate every time you read the newspaper, sort through your email, or listen to a colleague in a conversation.

In a dialogue, everyone deliberates between inquiry and advocacy: You *inquire* for more information or you *advocate* your own viewpoint. You shift between (a) asking questions/listening/summarizing, to (b) explaining your own viewpoint.[33]

GENERATIVE LISTENING

People like to think they can *multitask*. Neuroscience demonstrates that human beings have multitasked their brains into cognitive overload. This has depleted the human ability to focus. It has made people less efficient, not more.[34] Constant stimulation interferes with the brain's capacity to think creatively. It also prevents you from tapping into the wisdom that lies deep within you.[35]

One of the great myths of today's workplace is that you can save time by multitasking during a meeting. When everyone is multitasking, the meetings become a waste of everyone's time. When multitasking becomes the norm for meetings, the activity of leadership becomes impossible. Someone needs to step in to reinforce the norms we are discussing here.

If you are multitasking, and one of your tasks is listening, you are missing something. The interaction of leadership we describe in this book requires complete focus on that interaction. If you are participating in a leadership meeting, that interaction with other people requires your full, active, and conscious attention.

The first step in listening is to *be still*, to still the noise inside your head. A raging river does not allow anyone to see their own image. Only when the water becomes still can you see your reflection in a pool of water. In the same way, only when you become still (i.e., when you create *still waters* within you) can you see the reflections inside yourself. To be still is to separate yourself from the noise, to silence your own thoughts so you can find your focus in a conversation. It is only when you are quiet that you can truly listen.

In order to focus on *one* thing, you need to shut out the *many* things.[36] To be still helps you find your center, to shut out the past and the future so you can focus on the present. Thoughts about the argument you had this morning (the past) or the meeting that is coming up (the future) are obstacles to being fully present in the meeting that is happening now. To listen, you must devote your full attention to the present.

Generative listening means to open (1) your ears, (2) your mind, (3) your heart, and (4) your will.[37] First, open your ears by eliminating the external distractions. Second, open your mind by eliminating the internal distractions. Third, open your heart to identify with the emotional troubles of the other person(s). Fourth, open your will by being willing to change the way you act—based on what you are hearing.

Generative listening is critical for those engaged in adaptive leadership activities. Adaptive challenges demand a willingness and an openness to learn continuously, to understand the perspective of others, to benefit from the ideas of those closest to the adaptive problem, and to change attitudes, behaviors, and cultural norms.

GENERATIVE DIALOGUE

Generative dialogue occurs when people (1) eliminate the distractions so they can focus on each other with open ears; (2) eliminate the internal distractions so they can listen with open minds; (3) identify with the emotions behind the message with an open heart; and (4) hear the message and the emotions with an *open will* to change. The change occurs in the thoughts, the emotions, and ultimately in the actions of the group.

Dialogue is a *listen-and-summarize-and-respond* cycle: (1) You speak while I listen. (2) I summarize while you listen. (3) You clarify what I missed in my summary while I listen. (4) I acknowledge the clarifications you have made and respond to your ideas with my own ideas, while you listen. (5) You summarize while I listen. The dialogue continues with this cycle as others enter the dialogue when they listen, summarize, and respond.

A summary does not have to be long. It acknowledges the prior speaker, demonstrating respect and interest. It also allows the other person to clarify what may be misunderstood. This is what is meant by thinking together.[38] The listen-and-summarize-and-respond cycle lifts everyone to a higher understanding of the topic, while building trust across divisions.

Leadership requires communication in multiple directions. Leadership in this listen-and-summarize-and-respond cycle occurs in more than one voice. The role of leadership in a dialogue expands to virtually everyone because each person is influencing and being influenced by others at various points in the cycle. This is precisely what Joseph Rost means when he says that "leaders and followers do leadership together."[39]

Remember that leadership is not a person nor a position but an activity that involves leaders and followers. Dialogue allows for the practice of shared leadership. When someone takes the initiative, steps through the threshold of a new idea, and influences others to change their viewpoint, they are leading. Leaders become followers and followers become leaders.

To be in such a dialogue means you listen to more than one person. You listen to discern the *collective* will of the whole group. A dialogue sets out to discover *consensus*, or the sense of the group. A generative dialogue keeps the focus on the emerging consensus.

Listening during a dialogue does not mean simply staying quiet. Listening involves *mentally summarizing* what they are saying, *empathizing* with their emotional pain, and eventually, *asking* the right questions, with a facial expression and tone of voice that tunes into the other person. This is called *attunement*, which literally means you are "in tune" with the rest of the group. Attunement raises receptivity.

The most skillful leaders in a dialogue know how to wait and listen patiently as others express their views. They withhold judgment until a consensus begins to emerge, and they enter the dialogue by first summarizing what others are saying—preferably by quoting people *by name*—and then articulating the consensus.

CALL PEOPLE BY NAME

Calling someone by name is a sign of respect. When you truly respect someone, you learn their name. When you first hear someone's name, you let it sink in for a few seconds so you can remember their name. You immediately use their name. You call them by name and approach them as someone who can teach you. When you listen, you respect the *dignity* of that human person.

We have noticed that some of the leaders we admire the most tend to be the last ones to speak at a meeting. They enter a meeting with an open mind, hoping to understand what others think. They patiently suspend their own thoughts and ideas until they have devoted their total energy toward asking, listening, and summarizing. When they finally speak, others listen.

Look at it this way: When you are the first to speak, you cannot be sure the other people are ready to hear your message. They may be eager to share their own opinion. They may be busy rehearsing what they are going to say. They have low *receptivity*. They are not yet ready to receive your message. You can increase the receptivity of other people if you listen first. People are more likely to listen to you when and if you have listened to them.

CONCLUSION

Listening is a virtuous practice that is central to leadership for the greater good. It requires (1) wisdom to realize you don't have all the answers; (2) humility to admit that to others; (3) empathy to identify with the needs, interests, and emotions of the other person; (4) patience to endure the pain of someone else's burdens; and (5) mercy to act on what you learn.

In a globally changing and culturally complex world, dialogical skills have become more critical to leadership for the greater good. Misunderstandings can become disagreements that escalate into relational conflict that hurts our ability to work together. In the next chapter, we discuss how to address such conflict in the workplace.

CHAPTER 9

CONFLICT SKILLS

LEADING THROUGH CONFLICT

Like change, conflict is constant. If you are practicing adaptive leadership, conflict is inevitable. Leading change will generate conflict. Conflict is a daily occurrence for people who are interacting within a leadership relationship.

The key to growing conflict skills is to learn from past experiences by (1) embracing conflict mistakes as an opportunity for improvement, (2) reflecting on what happened, (3) remaining open to changing your mindset, and (4) seeing each conflict as something that is *normal* for human beings who are trying to do leadership together. Each day brings new conflicts that afford new opportunities to grow our conflict skills. Although each conflict is unique, there are certain skills that you can bring to each of them.

To learn from the past, you must live in the present (chapter 7). Yesterday's conflict becomes today's case study. It becomes today's topic for self-reflection. Once the painful experience subsides, you can find a moment to reflect before you make your next move. Many conflicts have several episodes before they are fully resolved.[1] Past emotions can spill over to present conflicts. Yesterday's painful memory can persevere. Yesterday's conflict can become today's nightmare when you avoid, stonewall, or do not address the conflict directly.

However, you can bring the conflict into the present through self-awareness. Awareness of your emotions—especially the ones that remain raw—and how they are affecting your present thoughts, intentions, and behaviors, can change the tone of your self-talk and improve your self-control (chapter 7). Each day brings a new opportunity to approach your conflicts differently if you can focus on the opportunity that is today.[2]

There are different *types* of conflict, and several *typologies* of conflict. The first is task conflict versus relationship conflict. *Task conflict* means that two or more people have a different approach to a task. They see the problem differently.

Research by Karen Jehn and others shows that small to moderate amounts of task conflict are healthy for teams and organizations.[3] Healthy task conflict allows a team to recognize the full range of perspectives needed to identify, analyze, and solve a problem. When task conflict is not present (or spoken), there is *groupthink*, which means everyone in the group is thinking the same way—which is not healthy for teams and organizations.[4]

Research also shows that even tiny amounts of *relationship conflict* are unhealthy for teams and organizations.[5] Relationship conflict occurs when people begin to attack each other instead of attacking the problem.[6] Research shows that relational conflict needs to be addressed—or it can destroy the trust that is needed for leadership.[7] Without attention to task conflict, relationship conflict tends to escalate.[8]

One way to deal with conflict is to *normalize* it. Simply admit the fact that conflict is *normal*. It occurs in every organization. It happens to everyone, every day. Imagine how boring a movie, a novel, or any story would be without conflict. Conflict is the stuff of life. The key is to deal with it as task conflict before it escalates into relationship conflict.[9]

FIVE APPROACHES TO CONFLICT

Kenneth Thomas presents five approaches to conflict, based on how assertive you are about meeting your own interests (concern for the task), and how cooperative you are in cooperating with the other person in the conflict to meet their interests (concern for the relationship).[10] As you can see in chart 12, four of the five responses to conflict align with the LTPS model we presented in chart 5 and all five of the behavioral styles in chart 4 (chapter 5).[11]

When you *compete* (Q1), the goal is to defeat the other parties in the conflict. Winning is everything and conversations quickly become a debate to convince others that you are right. In societies that are more individualistic, competition tends to be the most common approach to conflict. It is very common for those in authority, especially in authoritarian cultures, where the propensity is to tell and direct instead of to ask and collaborate.[12]

When you *accommodate* (Q3), the idea is to let the other person get whatever they want. For whatever reason, you just agree. Accommodation is a common approach for those without authority, especially in authoritarian cultures where people are expected to surrender to the higher authority, even when they

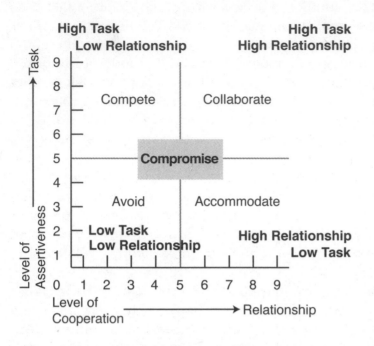

High Task
Low Relationship

High Task
High Relationship

Compete

Collaborate

Compromise

Avoid

Accommodate

**Low Task
Low Relationship**

**High Relationship
Low Task**

Task

Level of
Assertiveness

Level of
Cooperation

Relationship

Chart 12: Five Conflict Styles by Kenneth Thomas

adamantly disagree. Accommodation can also be an attempt to appease the other person, perhaps to make a friend or ally for the next disagreement. Another reason for accommodation is when someone does not care about the issue at hand.

When you *avoid* (Q2), you refuse to participate in efforts to discuss or address the conflict. You choose to look the other way and perhaps to harbor ill feelings about the conflict. This is not healthy for you or the other person. It can nurture hostility toward the other party. It can devolve into relationship conflict marred by passive aggressive behavior (which means passive on the task and aggressive on the relationship). As an approach that is low in concern for the task and low in concern for the relationship, it is the least effective approach for solving whatever task conflict is involved.[13]

When you *compromise*, you split the difference. Both parties get something, but neither gets what they really want or need. Compromise tends to work best in disagreements that can be measured, and when deadlines do not allow adequate time for collaboration. Whatever the split, what the two sides get typically adds up to 100 percent of what is being fought for. However, compromise means that *neither* party gets what they really want and need. Compromise can represent a failure to collaborate.

Each of these first four approaches has a certain flaw: (1) To compete is to have disregard for the relationship with the other person. (2) To accommodate is to demonstrate low concern for the task. (3) To avoid shows little or no regard for either the task or the relationship. (4) To compromise is to fail to imagine the possibilities of collaboration.

Nevertheless, Thomas says there are certain *situations* when you might want to compete, accommodate, avoid, or compromise—but only under some circumstances.[14] For example, when the other party is very aggressive, and the environment is competitive, you might need to become more competitive yourself, in order to meet the strong force of the other person. When the task is not your priority, and it is for others, you might want to be more agreeable. When tempers flare, it might be appropriate to avoid the conflict, but only temporarily, until cooler heads prevail. And when time is of the essence, or collaborative efforts have failed, compromise might be the best solution.

The fifth and optimal approach to conflict is *collaboration* (Q4). As the model shows, this approach is highest in concern for both the task and the relationship. To be collaborative means you are *assertive* about the task and *cooperative* on the relationship—at the same time. This is Q4 behavior.[15]

Collaboration is referred to as "principled negotiation" by Roger Fisher, William Ury, and Bruce Patton in *Getting to Yes*.[16] They highlight these four principles that accomplish "win-win" solutions: (1) separate the people from the problem; (2) focus on interests rather than positions; (3) generate a variety of options before settling on an agreement; and (4) insist that the agreement is based on objective criteria.

FIVE APPROACHES TO A CONFLICT

Let's say that you are applying for a promotion. In order to qualify for that promotion, your current boss needs to write a letter of support. Two weeks before the deadline, you approach your boss with a written proposal. Let's say that your boss supports the idea in concept but thinks your proposal is weak. Your boss has five options:

1. She can oppose the request and write a letter of opposition (Q1).
2. She can ignore the request and simply miss the deadline (Q2).
3. She can simply agree with your request and write a letter of support (Q3).
4. She can write a mixed message of both support and opposition (compromise).
5. She can collaborate with you to improve your proposal (Q4).

Option #5 (collaboration) is clearly her best choice. A collaborative conversation could strengthen your proposal, increase your odds for the promotion, and result in a healthier, more trusting relationship between you and your boss.

Option #1 (compete) would not be in your interest. You could fight her letter of opposition, but it would likely be a losing battle. Her decision to compete would hurt your cause for a promotion and your relationship with your boss.

Option #2 (avoid) would be just as harmful to your cause and your relationship with your boss. Without a letter from your boss, your application for promotion would be deemed incomplete and you would not have an opportunity to make your case for promotion. No one would read your application. Her lack of attention would cause resentment on your part, damaging your relationship. The passive aggressive nature of conflict avoidance is usually the worst possible scenario.

Option #3 (agree) may sound like it is in your interest but has a major flaw. If your boss has misgivings about your application for a promotion, it is in your interests to hear those concerns so you can address them. With her accommodation, you are not benefitting from her insights about how your proposal might have been improved, thus hurting your chances of the promotion. Even if you get the promotion, it would be better for you in the long run to be aware of her concerns. While accommodation may appear to improve (or not to harm) the relationship, it often fails because it lacks assertiveness on the task at hand.

Option #4 (compromise) may be preferable to competing, avoiding, or agreeing, but it also has flaws. You get a letter from your boss, but it sends a mixed message. The committee reading her letter is likely to have doubts about your qualifications for the promotion. Compromise should be a last resort only. It should be attempted only when collaboration is not possible, usually due to lack of time or resources. In this case, it would be much preferable for your boss to hold a conversation with you about her misgivings about your promotion.

Option #5 (collaboration), also called *principled negotiation*, is not only the most effective approach, it is healthier for all parties.[17] Any of the other options can be unhealthy for you, your boss, and your chances for a promotion. They are likely to harm the relationship and hurt your chances to advance your career.

CONFLICT MODEL

Conflict begins when you become aware that someone (the "other") has said or done something, or plans to do something, that jeopardizes something that you care about.[18] Immediately, *emotions* and *thoughts* flood your brain (chart 13). Your emotions affect your thoughts while thoughts affect your emotions (chapter 7).

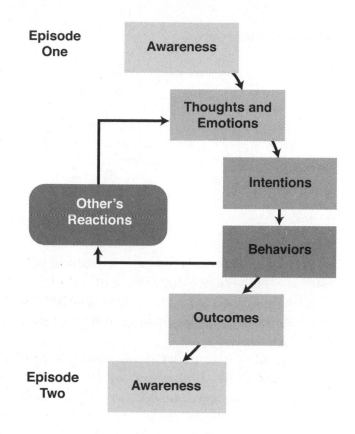

Chart 13: The Thomas Model of Conflict

Based on your thoughts and emotions, you develop *intentions* about how you will respond. Your intentions are not always consistent with your actions. They are simply what you intend to do. Following the five conflict styles described above, your intentions are either to compete, avoid, accommodate, compromise, or collaborate.[19]

Then you act. Your *actions* stir thoughts, emotions, and intentions on the part of the other person. The other person's perception of your action might be totally different from your intentions. Perhaps you had intended to collaborate, but the other person perceives your action as an attack.

Then the other person reacts to your action. That *reaction* stirs another round of thoughts, emotions, and intentions on your part. Your perception of the other person's action may be totally different from the other person's intentions. Perhaps that person intended to collaborate, but you perceived their response as an attack. You react. The other reacts to your reaction, and so on. This can go on for days, weeks, months, or even years.

Temperance is the virtue associated with controlling your "temper" or handling emotional distress. Temperance does not shut emotions out of brain activity. It gives emotions a balanced role that is proportionate to the situation. Emotions have a way of disturbing the brain's ability to process information.[20] Temperance restores that ability.

When you are edgy, nervous, or irritable, your physiological reaction to the situation is more likely to be interpreted by the other person as hostility, increasing the likelihood that they will also be on edge. Under these conditions, you are more likely to interpret the other person's behavior as a hostile attack, thus triggering more adrenaline and escalating the hormonal momentum in your brain. When you feel emotional distress, the tendency is to move quickly into action. Your thoughts and emotions get mixed together. In a heated environment, emotions tend to take over. Strong emotions can move you into autopilot. You lose your equilibrium, you lose your perspective, and you act without reason.[21]

When you become aware of a conflict, the tendency is to reflexively shift the focus of brain activity to the most primitive instincts—the hindbrain (the amygdala).[23] This limbic reflex is difficult to control. The amygdala signals you to be more self-centered, to be concerned only for your own basic survival and protection. This makes collaboration less likely.

Remember that adaptive leadership involves loss. It often entails negative emotions such as anger, fear, or sadness. To adapt is to change our attitudes, behaviors, or cultural norms. In any adaptive change, someone is asked to surrender something that is important to them. It might be a simple routine. It might involve a new set of relationships. Adaptive leadership acknowledges the loss and the emotions tied to that loss.

TIPS FOR HANDLING NEGATIVE EMOTIONS

Research shows that emotions are less powerful once they are named.[24] Naming emotions lowers the traumatic impact on the body. Perhaps this is because naming the emotion triggers self-awareness, which involves deeper parts of the human brain.

Reflective probes are statements that name the emotion you are noticing in the other person, for example, "You seem frustrated, what can I do to help?" Or "If that happened to me, I know that I would be upset."[25] Let's say the other person is angry. Their brain is releasing a chemical response from their sympathetic nervous system. Their heart rate increases. They lose oxygen in their blood stream. They can feel the anger in their gut.

At this point, nothing you say or do will change their physiological reaction. But you can do something that will gradually make an impact. You can help them obtain self-awareness by naming the emotion you are witnessing. This can increase the likelihood that they will be less destructive in their response. Research shows that just by validating their anger (for example), you can reduce the chemical response they are experiencing.[26]

A reflective probe helps the other person become aware of their emotional distress, thus triggering deeper parts of their brain. It reveals to the other person that their emotional reaction has become apparent to someone else. In many cases, the chemical reaction weakens in the other person. They become more self-aware. That self-awareness can change the self-talk occurring in their own mind. As a result, they are more likely to settle into a more objective view of reality.[27]

It is hard to underestimate the importance of self-awareness for both parties during a conflict. When a human being pauses, reflects, and becomes self-aware before making decisions and acting, the prefrontal lobes are playing a greater role in the decision-making process. From there, you can connect to the heart. This can trigger empathy. It can harmonize the head with the heart. When you become more conscious of the effect that emotions have on your actions and decisions, you can change your self-talk and become a happier and healthier human being.[28]

Self-reflection is key to this process. One person can face a very stressful situation and be overwhelmed with negative emotion. Another person might face a similar stressful situation, reflect on the experience, and change the self-talk in their mind. As the negative emotions lessen, the thoughts, ideas, and reactions can become more collaborative. You can grow in wisdom, which is nurtured by reflection on experience.

Perception can become reality. For example, if someone else perceives that you are being rude, then in that person's reality, you are being rude. It does not matter that you did not intend to be rude. It is the other person's perception of your actions that counts. Your job is to deal with that perception—especially when you are trying to perform leadership together. You can grow in empathy, which is nurtured by recognizing the thoughts and emotions of the other person.

To be human is to be emotional. To feel negative emotions like fear, anger, frustration, or jealousy is normal. The leadership challenge is to do something constructive with that emotion. It starts with identifying your own emotions, then to intuit the emotions of the other. Ask yourself, *Why am I afraid? Why am I angry? Why am I frustrated? Why am I jealous?* Also ask, *Why is this other person afraid, angry, frustrated, or jealous?* This takes mindful reflection.

Each conflict is an opportunity to learn and grow in wisdom and empathy.

THREE PATHWAYS TO COLLABORATION

Our colleague Randy Richards suggests that what path you take to resolve conflict depends on which of three types of conflict you are experiencing.[29]

An *interest conflict* occurs when two or more parties have opposing interests. They might be warring over scarce resources. In an interest conflict, you can often find common ground where both parties collaborate to get what they want or need. You look for what Fisher, Ury, and Patton call "options for mutual gain."[30]

A *factual conflict* happens when you have two different versions of what happened, or a disagreement about the facts in the case. It might be two different interpretations of a policy, procedure, or practice. In a factual conflict, you can often reach agreement by finding an expert source, or someone who is an expert, or an accepted policy that relates to the conflict. You look for what Fisher, Ury, and Patton call "objective criteria."[31]

A *normative conflict* materializes when attitudes, behaviors, values, or beliefs are in conflict.[32] Normative conflicts are at the heart of adaptive leadership. They can emerge out of a difference of opinion about (a) policies such as work schedules, (b) issues such as tardiness, (c) routines such as a weekly meeting, (d) priorities such as a budget, (e) values such as safety, (f) traditions such as a dress code, (g) strategies on how to resolve a problem, or (h) any behaviors that raise questions about *whether someone should be doing something.*

Normative conflicts are the most plentiful and the most difficult to resolve. They typically require more dialogue to come to a better appreciation for what each party values and why they behave as they do. Ask yourself,[33]

- What was the context of the other person's behavior?
- What choices did the other person have in that situation?
- Why did they choose to do what they did?
- What do you think would have been a better choice?
- Why do you think that is preferable?
- What should we do differently in the future?

After reflecting on open questions like these, sit down with the other person in the conflict and ask that person these very same questions. Try to see the conflict from their perspective. Remember that dialogue about a conflict is not a lecture. It is a conversation. Dialogue begins with an authentic desire to learn and grow from the conflict (chapter 8).

THE THREE-STEP MEETING

When you are engaged in conflict, try this three-step meeting[34] to resolve, contain, or navigate the conflict (chart 14):

First, ask the other person open questions to explore what the conflict looks like from their perspective (see above questions). In a conflict conversation, it is usually better to let the other person explain their perspective first. Listening will raise the receptivity of the other person. Generally, people are more interested in what you have to say once you have shown interest in what they have to say.

The Three-Step Meeting

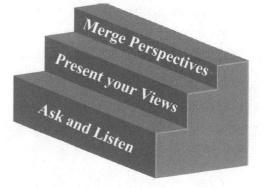

Chart 14: The Three-Step Meeting based on Randy Richards

Listen attentively. Listen with an open mind and open heart, where you can reflect on the other person's thoughts and emotions. If the other person is criticizing something that you have done, check your amygdala and consider the face value of that person's perspective. Think it through carefully. Be reflective of your emotions and theirs. Separate the other person from their criticism of your action.[35] Realize that when they describe your failure to do something, they are not saying that you are a failure. Weigh ideas truthfully and perspectives objectively.

Active, reflective, and responsive listening will increase their receptivity to listen to you. As they present their story, summarize their ideas, reflect their emotions, and ask, "Did I get that right?" "Is there anything else?" "How do you want me to help?" Once you have carefully listened to their story—and demonstrated this with accurate summaries and reflective probes—they are much more likely to listen to your story.

Second, explain your perspective. Be assertive about your needs and clear about your interests. Remember that collaboration requires that you are both assertive (high task) and cooperative (high relationship) at the same time. Try not to blame, exaggerate, or pronounce anything that will incite emotional distress on their part. Take some of the blame for the conflict. Acknowledge your mistakes. View your mistakes as lessons for the future, recognizing that mistakes today can make you better tomorrow, and accepting blame makes you easier to work with. To be human is to make mistakes.

Compliment the other person for something they said. Find areas of agreement with what they have shared. Point out that you both are committed to a mutual purpose or a common goal. Appeal to their higher instincts and you can help bring out the best version of that person.

Third, merge perspectives into a collaborative solution. Search for a common understanding of the conflict. Our colleague Randy Richards suggests that one way to accomplish this is by articulating a *neutral statement of the conflict*. This is a less adversarial and more collegial statement of what both parties agree is the essence of the conflict. Begin your neutral statement with, "The issue between us is…" or "Here is the problem we face together…."

Try to focus the conversation on solutions that meet the concerns of both parties. Take responsibility for meeting the other person's interest as if it is your own. Ask the other person,

Can you think of any ideas that might solve the problem for both of us?

What would it take for the two of us to get beyond this impasse?

If we had this to do all over again, how could we do things differently?

Solving the conflict in a way that benefits both parties will also serve to strengthen the relationship for the future. As Roger Fisher and Scott Brown point out, some of the closest working relationships are ones born of conflicts that were resolved amicably and collaboratively.[36] When you reach a solution that satisfies both the process concerns and the substance of the disagreement, you actually grow the relationship.

When you are engaged in the voluntary, interactive process of leadership, intending to affect real changes, you are certainly going to experience disagreements. It is part of your job as an adaptive leader to *orchestrate* the process of addressing these conflicts (chapter 1). At times, this means stimulating task conflict—without allowing it to escalate into relationship conflict. Your challenge is to navigate your way through conflict as you engage people to be involved in facing the reality of an adaptive challenge and leading the adaptive change that is in the best interests of both parties. This will take courage, patience, and resilience.

CONCLUSION

Methods for handling conflict are critical to the practice of leadership for the greater good. When you aspire to lead, you engage in voluntary, interactive relationships that intend real changes based on mutual purposes. The loss involved in adaptive leadership, and the inevitable conflict that it stirs up, can cause relationships to suffer. Collaborative approaches provide an opportunity to toughen your relationships, making them stronger and healthier than before the conflict occurred. Collaboration on one conflict can stimulate the virtuous cycle where trust grows and collaboration on the next conflict becomes more likely.

Leadership for the greater good requires facing the reality of adaptive challenges and practicing leadership together. This includes handling conflict together. Leadership and conflict go hand in hand. To lead through conflict means dealing in a healthy way with task conflict—which frequently exists but infrequently gets expressed—so that our disagreements pull us closer together rather than tearing us apart. Successfully managing task conflict can preserve, protect, and enhance the greater good for which you are striving.

CHAPTER 10

STRATEGIC SKILLS

STRATEGIC PLANNING

Strategy is the course of action taken to reach a goal or to fulfill mutual purposes. Strategy drives the adaptive change that is at the heart of leadership. *Strategic planning* is the formal process of determining that course of action. *Strategic thinking* is the informal process of reading the signs of the times, reflecting on changes in the world, and figuring out how to adjust, adapt and make strategic changes more spontaneously. Both are specific skills for leading adaptive change.[1]

We believe that to be consistent with our definition of leadership, strategic planning must be voluntary and interactive. It must employ influence tactics that intend adaptive changes. Therefore, our definition of *strategic planning* is *a voluntary, interactive process where leaders, followers, and managers develop strategies that intend adaptive change.* They cocreate strategic goals, strategies, action steps, and a shared vision.

The word *stratego* in Greek means "the general's view of the battlefield." That view was usually set atop a hill or mountain, where the general could gain a wholistic view of the action. In the industrial era, *strategic planning* was conducted as a *mountain-top retreat.* The most important people in the organization would spend several days developing a plan for the next five to ten years. They would come down from the mountain, like Moses with his Ten Commandments, and present the plan to their people.

Today, strategic planning is more like *whitewater rafting.* Everyone is in the same boat, moving swiftly down that mountain, steering their way through raging waters. Change is swirling around. People rely on each other at every twist and turn amidst the rocks, trusting each other to make quick decisions based on clear values, simple rules, and specific action steps.[2]

The *furious* pace of change in today's world does not fit well with the *glacial* pace of change within some organizations. Any organization today needs to adapt to the new reality of a world that comes at you like a freight train. In the postindustrial world, the leadership work of strategy involves more of the continuous strategic thinking and less of the formal strategic planning process. Nevertheless, strategic *planning* is still an essential skill for adaptive leadership. It also provides an opportunity to sharpen your strategic *thinking* skills.

Strategic planning is a conversation about the future. It is a process of listening and speaking about what matters most. In the process, people can get out of their comfort zone, become forward thinking, and develop the courage to take risks. They learn how to use *hindsight* to discover lessons from the past, *insight* to recognize the reality of the present, and *foresight* into what is coming next.[3]

Many people describe this as thinking *outside the box.* Note the box depicted in chart 15. It represents the "the way we have always done things," or "the usual way of doing things around here." These are the tired old strategies that people usually resort to when they face a new challenge. *Inside the box* means the same people doing the same things. To get outside the box, people must dismiss the notion that "we tried that before and it doesn't work."

As you think outside the box, you also need to think *inside the circle.* The circle represents the limits to which you can think outside the box. The limits in any business include

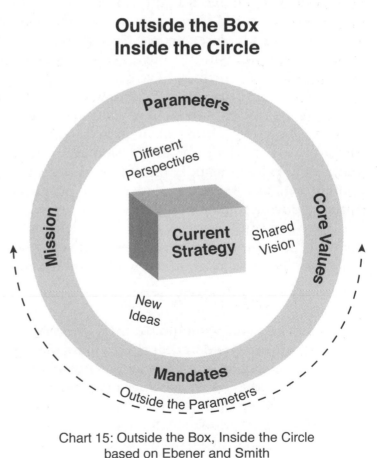

**Outside the Box
Inside the Circle**

Chart 15: Outside the Box, Inside the Circle
based on Ebener and Smith

company policies, core mission and values, government regulations, or other mandates. Every organization has a limit to how far outside the box it can think. But there is usually plenty of space *outside the box but inside the circle—* ground that has not yet been explored.[4]

Adaptive leadership requires *outside the box but inside the circle* thinking. Take for example the adaptive challenge of allowing for leadership to emerge from many directions. To change your mindset, you need to set aside your mistakes of the past and open your mind to future ways of thinking and acting. In today's fast-paced world, it is impossible for those in authority to have all the answers. It is naive to expect that.

The role of leadership is to generate the interaction and dialogue needed to solve the adaptive problem—not to come up with the answers themselves. Strategic planning can generate the synergy and tap into the *collective* experience of a team, producing ideas that could not be reached by any individual member.

Strategic planning can generate positive energy and enthusiasm for solving an adaptive challenge. It can be an opportunity for relationship building. Getting everyone on the same page helps build your team. Talking about mission and core values inspires people. Seeing change begin to happen builds a sense of hope and optimism. We have heard many people say to us at the end of a strategic planning session, "I've been through some very painful strategic planning before...but this was fun...and we got a lot done."

They are talking about our eight-step, *strategic planning process*, which Dan developed with our colleague Fred Smith (chart 16). The core values for this process are (1) a focus on mission and values, (2) active participation by as many stakeholders as possible, (3) interaction between the participants, (4) creation of a shared vision based on mutual purposes, and (5) continuous strategic thinking during implementation.

Here is a brief overview of our strategic planning process. For a full explanation of the interactive processes involved, check out *Strategic Planning: An Interactive Process for Leaders* by Dan Ebener and Fred Smith.

1. PLAN THE WORK

Before you can *work the plan* you must *plan the work* (or *plan to plan*). The most important consideration is how to involve as many members of your organization as possible. More participation gains two things:

First, it gathers a wider range of ideas. If everyone sees a problem the same way, the group is probably missing something. If everyone comes up with the same solution, the group may have *groupthink*.[5]

Second, more involvement creates more enthusiasm for the plan. When you are trying to get *buy*-in, it often means you are trying to *sell* something. The

The Ebener-Smith Strategic Planning Model

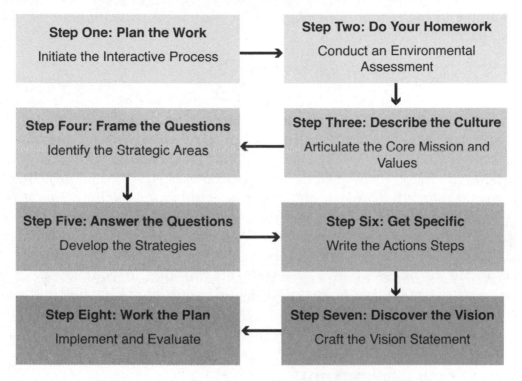

Step One: Plan the Work

Initiate the Interactive Process

Step Two: Do Your Homework

Conduct an Environmental Assessment

Step Four: Frame the Questions

Identify the Strategic Areas

Step Three: Describe the Culture

Articulate the Core Mission and Values

Step Five: Answer the Questions

Develop the Strategies

Step Six: Get Specific

Write the Actions Steps

Step Eight: Work the Plan

Implement and Evaluate

Step Seven: Discover the Vision

Craft the Vision Statement

Chart 16: The Ebener and Smith Strategic Planning Model

CEO and a few key people could write a strategic plan by themselves. It would be much easier. But it would be the plan only of a few people. Selling the plan is much easier when more people have participated in creating the plan. People buy into the change they choose.

PERSPECTIVE

If everyone looks at a chandelier on the ceiling of a room, each person sees the chandelier from their own unique perspective. No one sees the entire chandelier. To know what the other side of the chandelier looks like, someone needs to ask people who see it from that angle of the room. In strategic planning, you need to involve people from all corners of the organization if you want to get the full view of what is happening.

The other logistical issues involved with planning to plan include *where* and *when* to hold the planning sessions, *who* will facilitate, *how long* the sessions last, and *which* of the next steps to include in the process.[6] Generally, we recommend two, three-hour planning sessions, scheduled about two to six weeks apart.

2. DO YOUR HOMEWORK

Once you have established your plan to plan, it is time to begin to assess your environment. First, look *within* your organization and ask what is going well (your strengths), what could be better (your weaknesses), and how you could improve on those weaknesses. Second, look *outside* your organization and ask what changes in the world are creating opportunities for growth, challenges to that growth (threats), and how you could adapt to those changes.[7]

You might conduct a SWOT analysis, where you identify internal Strengths (S) and Weaknesses (W) and external Opportunities (O) and Threats (T). Strengths and weaknesses are factors *within* your control. Opportunities are trends in the business or in society that are working in your favor. Threats are big-picture trends that are working against your efforts. Opportunities and threats are *outside* your control.

INTERACTIVE PARTICIPATION

One way to maximize participation while doing your homework is to invite all members of the organization to engage in a focus group.[8] Gather their suggested strategies and ideas for improvement. You can also interview people who might have a unique perspective. For example, you might want to hold humble conversations with those closest to a problem (chapter 8). Have someone take careful notes of all the input. Then share the reports with the *strategic planning team*, which is those people who will attend the main planning sessions where the plan will be put together.

Make sure you find some way to invite all your people to offer their ideas and suggestions for improvement. This can be done through focus groups, interviews, or surveys. Involving lots of people who know the organization, including those working on the front lines of the company, can help you to identify your blind spots, the things you don't see.

3. REFLECT ON MISSION AND CORE VALUES

We usually start the first session of strategic planning with reflection on core mission and values, which reminds everyone of what is most important. Mission and values articulate the purpose and principles that should guide all decision-making, especially during strategic planning.[9]

The core of a mission statement is *purpose*. Every organization has a purpose. Ask yourselves, *What is your reason for being? Why do you exist? What is your nobler cause? What social benefit do you contribute to the common good? How does the work you do fulfill basic human needs?* That is your purpose.[10]

PURPOSE

Henry Ford was famous for speaking to purpose, which in his early days was to "democratize" the automobile. Steve Jobs stated his purpose as "making tools for the mind that advance humankind." Walt Disney said his purpose was "to make people happy."[11] What is common to these statements is they are short and sweet. A good purpose statement should quickly capture "the soul of the organization."[12]

The second part of a mission statement is called your *business*. Ask yourselves, *What do you do? What activities are at the core of your identity? What goods or services do you provide?* This part of a mission statement can be added to the purpose statement, often connected by a phrase such as "by providing...."[13]

The final part of the mission statement is core values, which are the basic precepts about what is most important in both business and life, and how business should be conducted.[14] The core values can be sprinkled into the mission statement. They can also be written as a separate document. The infamous *Johnson and Johnson Credo*, for example, written in 1943, reminds everyone that the first corporate responsibility is to the customer, then to the employee, to management, to the community, and last, to the shareholder.[15]

4. IDENTIFY STRATEGIC ISSUES

After reflecting on mission and values, we ask the strategic planning team to conduct their own environmental assessment, based on the results of the homework (step 2 above). We often use a process known as *snow cards* or

---

another called *conversation cafes*.[16] Both are interactive exercises to assess the environment and begin narrowing the priorities of the strategic plan (see *Strategic Planning for Leaders* for a longer explanation).[17]

Based on this assessment, the team makes the most critical decision of the strategic planning process: identifying the *strategic issues*. These are the most significant challenges—usually packed with plenty of adaptive challenge—facing your organization. They get articulated first as questions starting with "How can we…," and eventually they are reworded as your strategic goals.[18]

Strategic issues can be identified by studying the focus group reports, interviews, surveys, and other data gathered in the environmental assessment. They can also become apparent when studying the results of the environmental assessment conducted by the strategic planning team. We invite people to look at the results of their assessments and ask, *What strengths can you leverage to take advantage of our opportunities? What strengths will help you protect against your threats? What weaknesses need to be strengthened so you can act on your opportunities? What weaknesses need to be strengthened to protect against your threats?*

A STRATEGIC ISSUE

Let's say that one weakness in your business is that the core leaders are exhausted, and one opportunity in your SWOT is that new markets are opening. The strategic issue might be, *How can we develop new leaders who can develop new markets?*

Strategic issues are *important* but not necessarily perceived as *urgent*. For example, developing new leaders may be something that the organization has needed for years. It is important. But perhaps no one has created a sense of urgency about it.[19] Strategic planning demands that you become more strategic about your time and resources. It is time to refocus on the most important matters you are not addressing.

The key is to eliminate some of the things you are doing that are *urgent but not important*, so you can make time for those things that are *important but not urgent*. Your most difficult issues will not go away without refocusing your time and attention toward them. They demand new energy. They are screaming for someone to step up to practice leadership.

Typically, strategic issues are laden with adaptive challenges. Solutions are fleeting. Technical answers might provide partial solutions. However, if there was a technical solution to your strategic question, you probably would have applied it by now. Generally, strategic issues will require adaptive change in more than one area. They require a change in people's attitudes, norms, and behaviors. The tendency is to resort to technical fixes precisely because they are easy, or because the adaptive work will generate conflict.[20]

Unless you have a very large organization with plenty of untapped resources, it is best to limit your strategic issues to about three. Later you will be adding strategies to each strategic issue. You will also be adding action steps to each strategy, as depicted below (chart 17).[21] Strategic goals cascade into strategies that cascade into action steps.

5. DEVELOP STRATEGIES

Strategies are possible ways to answer the strategic questions raised in the previous step. Here we ask the groups to answer those questions—the ones

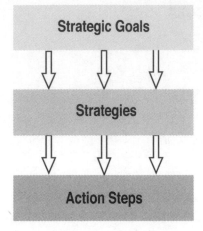

Chart 17: Ebener and Smith Model of Strategic Goals

that start with "How can we...?" We like to use *conversation cafes* to generate dialogue about strategies in a timely manner.[22] It is important to explore ways of addressing both the technical and adaptive aspects of each strategic issue.

Remember that strategic planning creates a safe space for risk taking—*inside the circle but outside the box*. All organizations have blind spots. Like junior partners in a law firm, new members in an organization can see things others might miss. Sharing those ideas will require trust, which can be built by practicing the active listening skills and collaborative negotiation skills we discussed in chapter 8.

6. CREATE AN ACTION PLAN

The *action plan* is what you will do in the first year of a strategic plan. It answers the question of *who is going to do what by when?* The key is specificity. The action plan sets the stage for later accountability and creates the support for future success.[23]

For each strategy identified above, write out three to four *action steps*. These are very specific things you will do to act on that strategy. The key is to articulate each step with enough specificity that you can hold yourself accountable in later months of the first year.

7. CAPTURE THE SHARED VISION

Many strategic planning models begin with stating a vision. Our experience suggests that when it is done that way, the vision is usually articulated by a charismatic person in the group. This is not the same as a *shared vision*. In our process, the shared vision is a *cocreation*.[24]

Most people confuse mission and vision. Mission is about purpose whereas vision is about direction. Mission is about the present, whereas vision describes the future. A vision is a beckoning symbol, a shining destination, or a distinctive path toward the future.[25] At the end of your strategic planning process, you can write an inspiring statement of the future by asking yourselves this vision question:

> *If we live out our mission, address our strategic issues, pursue our strategies, and take these action steps, what does the new world look like?*

Like a mission statement, a vision statement should be memorable and memorizable. It should paint a picture of what future success looks like. Our suggestion is to use an *external* vision statement, which focuses on how success would improve the world outside your business. An *internal* vision statement simply states how success would improve the business.[26] A vision statement should be inspiring to people inside and outside the organization. Once adopted, place it in front of the people to remind them of their targeted result.[27]

Remember that mission is about purpose, while vision focuses on direction. Vision changes as the world changes. Mission remains constant. More organizations struggle with vision than mission. They know their mission but do not know how to accomplish it. They have no plan. Without a plan, the vision fades.

Dialogue about vision is our last step in the final session of our formal process of strategic planning. Writing a vision statement, like the core values and mission statements, should be delegated to a small group, with one person designated as the primary author. Wordsmithing is not a large group activity.[28]

8. WORK THE PLAN

It never ceases to amaze us how many organizations spend hundreds of people hours in strategic planning but never implement the plan. We believe that "anything worth planning is worth doing—and anything worth doing is worth evaluating."[29] Once you have prepared, harnessed, and discerned the collective wisdom of the organization to determine what matters most, execute the plan by directing sufficient resources and focusing enough attention on your strategic issues.

Make your strategic plan the focus of your leadership team. The tendency is to breathe a sigh of relief, figure you got that done, and go back to business as usual. This is when leaders need to *create a sense of urgency about what is most important*. If you have decided that your strategic issues are the most critical issues facing the organization, they should dominate the agenda of your leadership meetings.

Make sure that all meetings focus on action. Keep reports to a minimum. Use a *consent agenda* (where minutes and reports are all approved in one motion, without oral review, unless there is a question about them). Expect people to read all reports before the meeting. At least once every three months, the strategic planning team should hold an accountability session to touch base, evaluate, and update the plan.

Strategic thinking is the ongoing work of strategic planning. Like a football coach who makes strategic adjustments when the wind changes directions or when a key player gets hurt, strategic leaders need to think strategically when changes occur or as progress unfolds.[30]

STRATEGY AND CULTURE

Organizational culture is the sum of our attitudes, values, customs, norms, beliefs, and behaviors.[31] Culture is the *normal* way of saying and doing things. It is your patterns of behavior, your ways of life. Culture has a direct impact on strategy and vice versa. You cannot make real progress on a strategic issue, or the adaptive challenges associated with it, until you begin to change the culture. Many organizational change models identify culture as the last thing that changes.[32]

People are more likely to *act themselves into a new way of thinking* than to think themselves into a new way of acting.[33] If your strategic goal involves changing your collective way of acting, it will take more than tending to action steps on a strategic plan to accomplish the change you wish to see.

TO BE WELCOMING

Let's say your strategic issue is, *How can we become more welcoming as an organization?* Some people think of welcoming as the job of a receptionist. That is a good start, but welcoming cannot stop at the front door. If you say your organization is welcoming, then you need to establish a sense of hospitality at the core of your culture.

To be welcoming is to be open, friendly, and outgoing. This can begin at the front door. But do you welcome new ideas from the new people whom you hire? How well do you welcome new ideas in your conversations and meetings? How often do you catch yourselves saying, hearing, or thinking, "We tried that before and it doesn't work."

Cultural change can happen from the *top down* or from the *bottom up*. Changing a tacit assumption or changing a cultural norm requires the work of those leading with and those leading without authority. Cultural change is an opportunity for anyone to lead.[34]

If you are going to *act yourselves into a new culture*, you need to do more than change your strategic plan. You will need to change attitudes and behaviors whenever the opportunity presents itself. You will need to change hearts and minds. That is the essence of leadership for the greater good. That is why leadership needs to be diffused throughout the organization. You cannot rely only on those in authority to do all the leading. They cannot be everywhere.

Culture is a major part of strategy. To act yourself into a new way of thinking and being, you need to change not only your strategy but also your culture. In fact, when addressing adaptive challenges, *the strategy can be the culture.*

STRATEGY AND STRUCTURE

All organizations rely on *structure*. It clarifies who is in charge, who is responsible for what, and who reports to whom. Structure allows for good management. It can also enhance or impede leadership. The problem develops when you don't breathe new life into old structures. The old paradigm was command and control with authority. The new paradigm is to inspire, to invite, and to influence—with or without authority.[35]

An unwieldy structure can suck the life right out of any organization by setting up multiple lines of approval to get things done. Structure can also create an illusion of control. You can establish rules that are considered "meant to be broken." Structure can also create the expectation that authorities will control certain behaviors that they cannot control. Control is about *extrinsic* motivation. Adaptive change requires *intrinsic* motivation.

Structure can dictate strategy. Strategy can dictate structure. Without structural support from the people in authority, a strategic plan will lack the resources or the attention to succeed. Without strategic support from the organization, those in authority will not change the attitudes, behaviors, and values inherent in an adaptive challenge. When addressing adaptive challenges, *the strategy can be the structure.*

CONCLUSION

Leadership in this increasingly complex world requires strategic planning and thinking skills. In a planning process, leadership for the greater good includes (1) creating the open space for strategic conversations, (2) ensuring that everyone has a voice in the process, (3) shifting the conversations toward adaptive instead of only technical issues, (4) insisting that disagreements are expressed and dealt with collaboratively, and (5) appealing to core mission, vision, and values.

Leadership for the greater good is an interactive activity. Therefore, the processes of leadership must also be interactive. Many of the dialogical, emotional, and conflict skills we discussed earlier will come into play as you conduct strategy sessions. When leading for the greater good, dialogical skills can ensure that all people are involved and all voices are heard in the strategic planning processes.

CONCLUSION

LEADING WITH AND LEADING WITHOUT AUTHORITY

Distinguishing leadership from authority does not diminish the need for authority. It simply creates another way of thinking about leadership. People can lead with or without authority. Working in hierarchical structures or authoritarian cultures may make it harder to lead because the standard is to control things in a top-down way. Of course, change can be dictated from the top—or from the outside. But this is not leadership.

Change can be dictated with a decree of a new policy or a new rule. It can be mandated by a new government policy. That change might even be necessary for the good of the community. The problem with dictating change is that you get less buy-in and more resistance. The challenge of leadership is to find more persuasive and less coercive ways to enact change.

Without change, there is no leadership. If you are not changing something, you are not leading. But dictating change is not leadership. Leadership is not coercive. Remember that leadership must be *voluntary* and *interactive*. If you are bullying people to get what you want, that makes you a bully, not a leader.

The tendency in most organizations is to train people in technical skills but not people skills. When people reach a certain level of experience, they are promoted into positions of authority. Universities create teachers who can become deans or principals. Boot camp produces privates who can become generals. Businesses hire engineers who become supervisors. And so forth.

Scanning the landscape of organizations, especially in this world that is changing so rapidly, we see the greatest need among leaders, managers, and followers is for people skills—not technical ones. If presented with an either/or choice, we think it is often better to hire people for their people skills and train them in technical skills, rather than the other way around.

THE ROLE OF AUTHORITY

The work of leadership for the greater good is enhanced when people in authority are *humble, patient, and merciful.*[1] They are humble about needing everyone's input to address adaptive issues, patient with the process of adaptive change, and merciful when risks taken do not always turn out right. Based on how they use their authority, they can either encourage or discourage others from taking the lead or participating in a change process.[2]

Warren Bennis and Burt Nanus suggest that people in authority can (1) become less reactive and more proactive, (2) move away from being the boss and toward becoming the coach, (3) focus less on supervision and more on empowerment, (4) delegate more responsibility to self-led teams, (5) be less responsible for training future managers and more concerned about training future leaders, and (6) be less worried about short-term profits and more focused on a long-term vision.[3]

As mentioned in our introduction, we think there is a direct connection between too much management and not enough leadership. When organizations are overmanaged, they most certainly will be underled. People in positions of authority can practice leadership for the greater good, and encourage it in others, when they make the switch from a relationship based on authority to one based on mutual influence. To make this switch is a risk worth taking because it can catapult your people into practicing leadership.[4]

Remember that to lead when you have positional authority, you must resist the temptation to rely so heavily on that authority. Leading with authority requires that you set aside that very authority. To lead when you have authority, imagine that you do not have that authority. Paradoxically, leading with authority is influencing without using your authority.

THE COURAGE TO LEAD

Think of it this way: leadership *without* authority can occur in one of two ways. Either (a) you have positional authority but choose not to use it, or (b) you lack positional authority altogether. In our experience, the first option is less common. The second option releases you from the temptation to use your positional authority because you have none. Therefore, you have no choice but to rely on the voluntary, interactive nature of leadership: to ask questions, listen, and dialogue (chapter 8).

When you lead without authority, your influence tactics are based on intrinsic motivators. Your lack of positional authority also allows free reign for leaders and followers to exchange positions and take turns with practicing leadership.

It takes *courage, patience, and resilience* to influence when you have no formal authority. As Heifetz points out, it can be dangerous to initiate action on adaptive issues because most people are comfortable with the status quo and would rather avoid the conflict involved in adaptive work.[5] The process of adaptive leadership without authority can take much longer because nonpositional leaders lack the access to resources that are afforded to those with authority. They must be in it for the long haul.

Allan Cohen and David Bradford suggest that it is an illusion that people think they can command and control their teams into success.[6] To think that managers just need to give clear directions and ensure compliance with orders that get carried downward through the organization is an old idea. There is never enough positional power to get everything done. They suggest that it is only by having the courage to lead without authority that managers can succeed.

The bottom line is that people can lead *with or without* authority, but no organization can go *with or without* leadership. Organizations need leadership to adapt to the external changes so prevalent in today's world. Organizations need change. Therefore, they need more leadership—leadership that can emerge from anywhere—and less command-and-control authority. Leadership for the greater good can intrinsically motivate people to be fully engaged.

Organizations need both leadership *and* management. Managers develop structure in organizational lives. Leaders breathe life into organizational structures. Adaptive change will require courage from both leaders and managers. It requires an appeal to the sense of purpose that creates meaning in people's lives, such as the meaning invoked by the greater good.

Leadership will emerge when people search their hearts and ask, "What needs to be changed?" When you answer that question, perhaps the sense of purpose connected to that change can supply you with the *courage to lead*—so you can take the initiative when the moment arises to lead for the greater good.

AFTERWORD

RANDY RICHARDS AND RON WASTYN

Almost all writing about organizational leading and managing assumes the traditional industrial hierarchical structure. That structure, symbolically represented as the org chart pyramid, designates an order based on ascending levels of authoritarian command and control. It emerged over time when what organizations wanted from employees was simply to do what people in positions of authority told them to do. Management had all the answers. The whole point of this form of hierarchy is to tell and control each level beneath what the level above them expected them to do. Most often not just "what," but also "how." Perhaps this reached its culmination with Ford and Taylor. Such organizations became highly efficient and productive.

However, it became increasing, if grudgingly, apparent that management did not have all the answers. If we might borrow a concept from economics, organizational hierarchies based on command and control generate several undesirable externalities. Demanding that people do as they are told, or else, creates workplaces where fear is ever present. Fear is a significant barrier for organizational thriving. Command-and-control methods discourage initiative as each level waits for instructions from above on the what and the how. Knowledge gained at levels below remains there because information in a command-and-control structure flows down, not up. Each level up, therefore, is making decisions with insufficient information, increasing the likelihood of mistakes and missed opportunities. The natural tendency is to resist being controlled and to assert oneself. If this resistance will not be tolerated openly, then various forms of passive aggressive behavior evolve, stymieing even positive attempts at organizational operations.

These negative consequences and others became more and more apparent in the postwar years of the twentieth century. In order to compensate for the structurally generated problems of command and control, several suggested reforms emerged. Most notably, Toyota made its breakthrough methods of *kaizen*. The Toyota Way example helped generate the Total Quality Management movement and Quality Circles. On the management philosophy side, McGregor's Theory X and Theory Y helped legitimate softening the hard edges of command-and-control hierarchies.

In one way or another, most of the leadership literature today is spinning out various iterations of Theory Y (that people are self-motivated). These efforts aim at undoing or softening the harsh realities of working life in command-and-control hierarchies. If we use McGregor's work at Sloan as an anchor point, these attempts to mitigate the negative externalities of command-and-control organizational hierarchies have been going on for nearly seventy years! Evidently, to little avail. The same Theory Y assumptions, values, and mentality that McGregor described in the 1950s as an antidote to the Theory X mentality (that people have little ambition) keep appearing in all manner of publications, training programs, and consulting as what leadership is really all about. Perhaps the very structure of command-and-control hierarchies inevitably generates these negative outcomes that no one really wants. If so, then it is time to consider another form of structure and hierarchy, not one based on command and control with power emanating top down. Once we do that, the conversation around leadership may be significantly altered.

Fredric Laloux's book *Reinventing Organizations* challenges, with specific successfully functioning organizations, the necessity of command-and-control hierarchies. Laloux's work demonstrates that across a variety of different kinds of organizations (which Laloux calls "Teal organizations"), it is not necessary to have a separate group of people to tell others what to do. It is the end of management as a class. He describes several organizations that function quite successfully without bosses.

Without any bosses, no one can make anyone do anything. All activity in that sense becomes a matter of voluntary influence. Under Rost and some theories, this would count as "leadership" on the sole basis of it being voluntary and not commanded. However, if this were true, then there would be no managing in these Teal organizations. There would be only leadership. Of course, this is nonsense because everyone is managing. However, it does expose the flaw in such an understanding of leadership, even in the traditional organizations where managers often do influence and persuade.

Now, all employees are people in positions of authority with the power to make decisions (using some form of the advice method). Everyone has organizational authority. If everyone is a manager, and if managers can only use voluntary influence with others, and if anyone can make any organizational decision so long as they follow the advice process, then how are we to understand "leadership"? To put it another way, what distinguishes "managing" from "leading" in these Teal organizations?

We think the distinction made by the adaptive leadership folks (such as Ronald Heifetz and Marty Linsky) still holds. Whenever organizational associates are engaged in running the day-to-day operations or solving *technical* problems, then we can say they are managing. Whenever organizational associates are engaged in addressing *adaptive*/cultural issues, then we can say they are leading.

Dr. Randy Richards is professor emeritus at St. Ambrose University.
Dr. Ron Wastyn is professor of organizational leadership
at St. Ambrose University.

APPENDIX
TIPS FOR FACILITATING A DIALOGUE

If you are facilitating a dialogue, here are some questions to ask yourself about the interactive dynamics—and interventions you might want to attempt:

Do people *pause* long enough after a good question is asked—so that the reflective ones in the group have enough time to respond? If not, call on the quieter ones to give them a chance to talk.

Are people using *eye contact* and nodding to the person who is speaking? If not, perhaps they are beginning to disengage. Get the dialogue back on topic by asking an open question or call on some new voices to get involved.

Are participants beginning to *speak over* each other's voices? If so, ask the next person who speaks to restate what the previous person has said before making their own comment.

Is anyone dominating the conversation while others are drifting away? If so, make a comment such as, "Thanks for sharing, Bill. Now let's hear what some others have to say about this....Paula, what do you think about X?"

If two people begin speaking at the *same time*, what happens to the person who paused to allow the other to speak? Does she or he get lost in the rotation of speakers? If so, call on that person and ask if they have something to contribute.

Is someone in the group getting edgy? Angry? Frustrated? Use a *reflective probe* to draw out that person. Make a comment such as, "You seem to be upset about this. Can you help us understand this from your perspective?"

Are two or three people turning the dialogue into a *debate*? If so, ask each side to summarize what the other side is saying. When the summary is expressed, ask the other side to clarify anything that might be absent or misleading from the summary.

Are people asking *loaded* questions, or *leading* questions, ones that suggest one "right" answer? If so, reframe the question as open-ended, such as, "How can we get this done? What are some of the options available to us?"

Are people showing empathy toward others who have a viewpoint different than theirs? If not, make empathetic comments of your own. Say, "I get it. You are frustrated. How can we help?" Or "I understand that you are upset about this. What would you like us to do?" Model the communication skills you want to see.

A facilitator must be able to read the emotions and hear the statements that are not necessarily being expressed out loud. Reach out to those who are upset.

Postscript: Even when you are not formally the facilitator of a meeting, you can improve the quality and the flow of interaction by practicing the suggestions above. Let's say someone is trying to present an idea but someone else interrupts—and the facilitator does not say anything. Later, you might ask the person who was interrupted to finish presenting their idea. You could say, "Maria, you didn't get a chance to finish what you were saying a few minutes ago. I'm curious, what else were you going to say?"

With or without authority, *anyone* can lead a meeting. Anyone can make everyone a bit more conscious about the group dynamics. Anyone can turn a debate into more of a dialogue. Anyone can reduce the number of interruptions—which are forceful ways to steal attention away from someone else. If left unchallenged, interruptions can become part of the culture of a group. They can become so habitual that they are hardly noticed. The key is to call them out before they become routine. In the process, you are changing the culture of the meeting.

NOTES

PREFACE

1. Robert K. Greenleaf, *Servant Leadership: A Journey into the Nature of Legitimate Power and Greatness* (New York: Paulist Press, 1977).

2. Joseph C. Rost, *Leadership for the Twenty-First Century* (New York: Praeger, 1991).

3. Allan R. Cohen and David L. Bradford, *Influence without Authority*, 2nd ed. (Hoboken, NJ: Wiley, 2005).

4. Dan R. Ebener, *Blessings for Leaders: Leadership Wisdom from the Beatitudes* (Collegeville, MN: Liturgical Press, 2012).

5. Ronald A. Heifetz, Alexander Grashow, and Martin Linsky, *The Practice of Adaptive Leadership: Tools and Tactics for Changing Your Organization and the World* (Boston: Harvard Business Press, 2009).

6. Jeffrey A. Barach and D. Reed Eckhardt, *Leadership and the Job of the Executive* (Westport, CT: Quorum Books, 1996).

7. Ronald A. Heifetz and Martin Linsky, *Leadership on the Line: Staying Alive through the Dangers of Leading* (Boston: Harvard Business School Press, 2002).

8. Kenneth Wayne Thomas, *Intrinsic Motivation at Work: Building Energy and Commitment* (San Francisco: Berrett-Koehler, 2002).

9. Rost, *Leadership for the Twenty-First Century.*

10. Daniel Goleman, *Emotional Intelligence* (New York: Bantam Books, 2005).

11. Edgar H. Schein, *Humble Inquiry: The Gentle Art of Asking Instead of Telling* (San Francisco: Berrett-Koehler, 2013).

12. Randy L. Richards, *Conflict and Collaboration: The Search for the Integrative Space* (Rock Island, IL: Richards, 2017).

13. Dan R. Ebener and Frederick L. Smith, *Strategic Planning: An Interactive Process for Leaders* (Mahwah, NJ: Paulist Press, 2015).

INTRODUCTION: LEADERSHIP AND MANAGEMENT

1. John P. Kotter, *Leading Change* (Boston: Harvard Business School Press, 1996).

2. Joseph C. Rost, *Leadership for the Twenty-First Century* (New York: Praeger, 1991).

PART I: LEADERSHIP TODAY

INTRODUCTION

1. D. Scott Derue and Susan J. Ashford, "Who Will Lead and Who Will Follow? A Social Process of Leadership Identity Construction in Organizations," *The Academy of Management Review* 35, no. 4 (2010): 627–47, esp. 627.

2. D. Scott DeRue, "Adaptive Leadership Theory: Leading and Following as a Complex Adaptive Process," *Research in Organizational Behavior* 31 (January 2011): 125–50, esp. 126, https://doi.org/10.1016/j.riob.2011.09.007.

3. James M. Kouzes and Barry Z. Posner, *The Leadership Challenge: How to Make Extraordinary Things Happen in Organizations*, 6th ed. (Hoboken, NJ: Leadership Challenge, 2017).

4. Ronald A. Heifetz, *Leadership without Easy Answers* (Cambridge, MA: Belknap Press of Harvard University Press, 1994).

CHAPTER 1: THE TASK OF LEADERSHIP

1. Joseph C. Rost, *Leadership for the Twenty-First Century* (New York: Praeger, 1991), 102.

2. Rost, *Leadership for the Twenty-First Century*.

3. Rost, *Leadership for the Twenty-First Century*.

4. Rost, *Leadership for the Twenty-First Century*, 115.

5. Rost, *Leadership for the Twenty-First Century*.

6. Peter Guy Northouse, *Leadership: Theory and Practice*, 6th ed. (Thousand Oaks, CA: SAGE, 2013).

7. James MacGregor Burns, *Leadership* (New York: Harper & Row, 1978).

8. Ronald A. Heifetz, Alexander Grashow, and Martin Linsky, *The Practice of Adaptive Leadership: Tools and Tactics for Changing Your Organization and the World* (Boston: Harvard Business Press, 2009).

9. Juan Carlos Eichholz, *Adaptive Capacity: How Organizations Can Thrive in a Changing World* (Greenwich, CT: LID, 2014), 10.

10. Ronald A. Heifetz and Marty Linsky, "A Survival Guide for Leaders," *Harvard Business Review*, June 2002.

11. Ronald A. Heifetz and Martin Linsky, *Leadership on the Line: Staying Alive through the Dangers of Leading* (Boston: Harvard Business School Press, 2002).

12. Heifetz and Linsky, "Survival Guide for Leaders."

13. Elisabeth Kübler-Ross, *On Death and Dying: What the Dying Can Teach Doctors, Nurses, Clergy and Their Own Families* (New York: Scribner, 1969).

14. Margaret Wheatley, "Some Friends and I Started Talking," *DailyGood News That Inspires* (blog), January 7, 2014, http://www.dailygood.org/story/614/some-friends-and-i-started-talking/.

15. Edward M. Kennedy, "Eulogy for Robert Kennedy," *New York Times*, June 9, 1968.

16. Leon C. Megginson, "Lessons from Europe for American Business," *The Southwestern Social Science Quarterly* 44, no. 1 (June 1963): 3–13.

17. Ronald A. Heifetz, *Leadership without Easy Answers* (Cambridge, MA: Belknap Press of Harvard University Press, 1994).

18. Heifetz, Grashow, and Linsky, *Practice of Adaptive Leadership*, 19.

19. Ronald A. Heifetz and Donald L. Laurie, "The Work of Leadership," *Harvard Business Review*, February 1997.

20. Heifetz, Grashow, and Linsky, *Practice of Adaptive Leadership*.

21. Adapted from Heifetz and Laurie, "The Work of Leadership"; Heifetz and Linsky, *Leadership on the Line*.

22. Heifetz, *Leadership without Easy Answers*.

23. Heifetz, Grashow, and Linsky, *The Practice of Adaptive Leadership*.

24. Heifetz and Linsky, *Leadership on the Line*.

25. Michael J. Marquardt, *Leading with Questions: How Leaders Find the Right Solutions by Knowing What to Ask*, rev. and updated ed. (San Francisco: Jossey-Bass, 2014), 154.

26. Eichholz, *Adaptive Capacity*.

27. Heifetz, Grashow, and Linsky, *Practice of Adaptive Leadership*.

28. Heifetz and Linsky, *Leadership on the Line*.

29. Dan R. Ebener and Frederick L. Smith, *Strategic Planning: An Interactive Process for Leaders* (Mahwah, NJ: Paulist Press, 2015), 93.

30. Edgar H. Schein, *Humble Inquiry: The Gentle Art of Asking Instead of Telling* (San Francisco: Berrett-Koehler, 2013).

31. Schein, *Humble Inquiry*, 57.

32. Heifetz, Grashow, and Linsky, *Practice of Adaptive Leadership*.

33. Heifetz and Linsky, *Leadership on the Line*.

34. Lee G. Bolman and Terrence E. Deal, *Reframing Organizations: Artistry, Choice, and Leadership*, Jossey-Bass Management Series (San Francisco: Jossey-Bass, 1991).

35. Heifetz and Linsky, "Survival Guide for Leaders."

36. Heifetz and Linsky, *Leadership on the Line*.

37. John P. Kotter, *A Sense of Urgency* (Boston: Harvard Business Press, 2008).

38. Heifetz and Linsky, *Leadership on the Line*.

39. Heifetz and Linsky, *Leadership on the Line*.

40. Schein, *Humble Inquiry.*

41. Eichholz, *Adaptive Capacity.*

42. Heifetz and Linsky, *Leadership on the Line.*

43. Rost, *Leadership for the Twenty-First Century.*

44. Heifetz and Linsky, *Leadership on the Line.*

45. Heifetz and Linsky, *Leadership on the Line.*

46. Eichholz, *Adaptive Capacity*, 104.

47. Eichholz, *Adaptive Capacity*, 41.

48. Heifetz and Linsky, *Leadership on the Line.*

49. Eichholz, *Adaptive Capacity.*

CHAPTER 2: THE RELATIONSHIP OF LEADERSHIP

1. Joseph C. Rost, *Leadership for the Twenty-First Century* (New York: Praeger, 1991), 102.

2. Rost, *Leadership for the Twenty-First Century.*

3. Rost, *Leadership for the Twenty-First Century*, 112.

4. John French and Bertram Raven, "The Bases of Social Power," in *Studies in Social Power*, ed. Dorwin Cartwright (Ann Arbor: Research Center for Group Dynamics, Institute for Social Research, University of Michigan, 1959), 150–57.

5. Don Cohen and Laurence Prusak, *In Good Company: How Social Capital Makes Organizations Work* (Boston: Harvard Business School Press, 2001).

6. Afsaneh Nahavandi, *The Art and Science of Leadership*, 4th ed. (Upper Saddle River, NJ: Pearson/Prentice Hall, 2006).

7. James M. Kouzes and Barry Z. Posner, *The Leadership Challenge: How to Make Extraordinary Things Happen in Organizations*, 6th ed. (Hoboken, NJ: Leadership Challenge, 2017).

8. Mary Parker Follett, *Freedom and Co-ordination: Lectures in Business Organization* (London: Routledge, 2015).

9. Rost, *Leadership for the Twenty-First Century.*

10. Rost, *Leadership for the Twenty-First Century,*111.

11. Rost, *Leadership for the Twenty-First Century.*

12. Kenneth Wayne Thomas, *Intrinsic Motivation at Work: Building Energy and Commitment* (San Francisco: Berrett-Koehler, 2002).

13. Thomas, *Intrinsic Motivation at Work.*

14. Terrence E. Deal and Allan A. Kennedy, *Corporate Cultures: The Rites and Rituals of Corporate Life* (Cambridge, MA: Perseus, 2000).

15. Thomas, *Intrinsic Motivation at Work.*

16. Rost, *Leadership for the Twenty-First Century*, 106.

17. Ralph K. White and Ronald Lippitt, *Autocracy and Democracy: An Experimental Inquiry* (Westport, CT: Greenwood Press, 1972).

18. Charles C. Manz and Henry P. Sims, *Business without Bosses: How Self-Managing Teams Are Building High-Performing Companies* (New York: Wiley, 1995).

19. Daniel H. Pink, *Drive: The Surprising Truth about What Motivates Us* (New York: Riverhead Books, 2011); Nikolaos Dimitriadis and Alexandros Psychogios, *Neuroscience for Leaders: A Brain Adaptive Leadership Approach* (London: Kogan Page, 2016).

20. Thomas, *Intrinsic Motivation at Work*; Bernard M. Bass and Ralph M. Stogdill, *Bass & Stogdill's Handbook of Leadership: Theory, Research, and Managerial Applications*, 3rd ed. (New York: Free Press, 1990).

21. Thomas, *Intrinsic Motivation at Work*.

22. Nick Craig, *Leading from Purpose* (New York: Hachette, 2018).

23. James C. Collins and Jerry I. Porras, "CMR Classics: Organizational Vision and Visionary Organizations," *California Management Review* 50, no. 2 (January 2008): 117–37, https://doi.org/10.2307/41166438.

24. Richard M. Ryan and Edward L. Deci, "Overview of Self-Determination Theory: An Organismic-Dialectical Perspective," in *Handbook of Self-Determination Research*, ed. E. L. Deci and R. M. Ryan (Rochester, NY: University of Rochester Press, 2002), 5.

25. Kirk Warren Brown and Richard M. Ryan, "The Benefits of Being Present: Mindfulness and Its Role in Psychological Well-Being," *Journal of Personality and Social Psychology* 84, no. 4 (2003): 822–48, https://doi.org/10.1037/0022-3514.84.4.822.

26. Thomas, *Intrinsic Motivation at Work*.

27. Edward L. Deci, *Intrinsic Motivation* (Boston, MA: Springer US, 1975), https://doi.org/10.1007/978-1-4613-4446-9; Ryan and Deci, "Overview of Self-Determination Theory," 7.

28. Deci, *Intrinsic Motivation*; Ryan and Deci, "Overview of Self-Determination Theory," 7.

29. Edward L. Deci and Richard M. Ryan, "The 'What' and 'Why' of Goal Pursuits: Human Needs and the Self-Determination of Behavior," *Psychological Inquiry* 11, no. 4 (October 2000): 227–68, https://doi.org/10.1207/S15327965PLI1104_01.

30. Bass and Stogdill, *Bass & Stogdill's Handbook of Leadership*.

31. Edward L. Deci and Richard M. Ryan, "The Support of Autonomy and the Control of Behavior," *Journal of Personality and Social Psychology* 53, no. 6 (1987): 1024–37, https://doi.org/10.1037/0022-3514.53.6.1024.

32. Ryan and Deci, "Overview of Self-Determination Theory."

33. Richard M. Ryan and Edward L. Deci, "Self-Regulation and the Problem of Human Autonomy: Does Psychology Need Choice, Self-Determination, and Will?" *Journal of Personality* 74, no. 6 (December 2006): 1557–86, https://doi.org/10.1111/j.1467-6494.2006.00420.x.

34. Richard M. Ryan, Julius Kuhl, and Edward L. Deci, "Nature and Autonomy: An Organizational View of Social and Neurobiological Aspects of Self-Regulation in Behavior and Development," *Development and Psychopathology* 9, no. 4 (December 1997): 701–28, https://doi.org/10.1017/S0954579497001405.

35. Dennis W. Organ, Philip M. Podsakoff, and Scott Bradley MacKenzie, *Organizational Citizenship Behavior: Its Nature, Antecedents, and Consequences*, Foundations for Organizational Science (Thousand Oaks: SAGE Publications, 2006).

36. Dennis W. Organ, *Organizational Citizenship Behavior: The Good Soldier Syndrome*, Issues in Organization and Management Series (Lexington, MA: Lexington Books, 1988).

37. Organ, Podsakoff, and MacKenzie, *Organizational Citizenship Behavior*.

38. Organ, Podsakoff, and MacKenzie, *Organizational Citizenship Behavior*.

39. Organ, Podsakoff, and MacKenzie, *Organizational Citizenship Behavior*.

40. Organ, Podsakoff, and MacKenzie, *Organizational Citizenship Behavior*.

41. Dan R. Ebener, *Servant Leadership Models for Your Parish* (Mahwah, NJ: Paulist Press, 2010).

42. Robert K. Greenleaf et al., *The Servant-Leader Within: A Transformative Path* (Mahwah, NJ: Paulist Press, 2003).

43. Dan R. Ebener, *Pastoral Leadership: Best Practices for Church Leaders* (Mahwah, NJ: Paulist Press, 2018).

44. Dan R. Ebener, "On Becoming a Servant Leader," *Sojourners*, February 2011.

45. Greenleaf et al., *Servant-Leader Within*.

46. Peter F. Drucker, *Management: Tasks, Responsibilities, Practices* (New York: HarperBusiness, 1993).

47. Robert K. Greenleaf, *Servant Leadership: A Journey into the Nature of Legitimate Power and Greatness* (Mahwah, NJ: Paulist Press, 1977).

48. Greenleaf et al., *Servant Leadership*.

49. Greenleaf et al., *Servant Leadership*.

50. Ebener, *Servant Leadership Models for Your Parish*.

51. Thomas, *Intrinsic Motivation at Work*.

CHAPTER 3: THE ETHICS OF LEADERSHIP

1. An example of such approach can be seen in the work of Joanne B. Ciulla et al., "Guest Editors' Introduction: Philosophical Contributions to Leadership Ethics," *Business Ethics Quarterly* 28, no. 1 (2018): 1–14, https://doi.org/10.1017/beq.2017.48.

2. An example of such an approach can be seen in Robert S. Rubin, Erich C. Dierdorff, and Michael E. Brown, "Do Ethical Leaders Get Ahead? Exploring Ethical Leadership and Promotability," *Business Ethics Quarterly* 20, no. 2 (April 2010): 215–36, https://doi.org/10.5840/beq201020216.

3. We are not referring to the "extreme case approach," as Price calls it. In other words, we are not focusing on the best or worst examples of leaders, but we are talking about specific types of cases that will raise awareness on the ethical intricacies of the process of leadership. See Terry L Price, *Leadership Ethics: An Introduction* (Cambridge: Cambridge University Press, 2008).

4. Joanne B. Ciulla, "Leadership Ethics: Mapping the Territory," *Business Ethics Quarterly* 5, no. 1 (January 1995): 5–28, https://doi.org/10.2307/3857269.

5. Ciulla, "Leadership Ethics."

6. Michael Beer, Magnus Finnstrom, and Derek Schrader, "Why Leadership Training Fails—and What to Do About It," *Harvard Business Review*, October 2016, 50–57.

7. Norman E. Bowie, "Expanding the Horizons of Leadership," in *The Quest for Moral Leaders: Essays on Leadership Ethics*, ed. Joanne B. Ciulla, Terry L. Price, and Susan E. Murphy (Northampton, MA: Edward Elgar, 2005), 144–60.

8. C. A. J. Coady, "The Problem of Dirty Hands," in *The Stanford Encyclopedia of Philosophy*, ed. Edward N Zalta (Stanford, CA: Metaphysics Research Lab, Stanford University, 2018), https://plato.stanford.edu/archives/fall2018/entries/dirty-hands/.

9. Joanne B. Ciulla, "Leadership Ethics," in *International Encyclopedia of Ethics* (Oxford, UK: John Wiley & Sons, Ltd, 2017), 1–7, https://doi.org/10.1002/9781444367072.wbiee370.pub2.

10. In our treatment of philosophical ethics, we are very much relying on Damir Mladic's approach to the subject in his lectures and publications.

11. David Knights and Majella O'Leary, "Leadership, Ethics and Responsibility to the Other," *Journal of Business Ethics* 67, no. 2 (2006): 125–37.

12. Robert Johnson and Adam Cureton, "Kant's Moral Philosophy," in *The Stanford Encyclopedia of Philosophy*, ed. Edward N. Zalta (Stanford, CA: Metaphysics Research Lab, Stanford University, 2019), https://plato.stanford.edu/archives/spr2019/entries/kant-moral/.

13. Elizabeth Haas Edersheim and Peter F. Drucker, *The Definitive Drucker* (New York: McGraw-Hill, 2007).

14. James MacGregor Burns, *Leadership* (New York: Harper & Row, 1978).

PART II: THE TRADITIONAL THEORIES

INTRODUCTION

1. Joseph C. Rost, *Leadership for the Twenty-First Century* (New York: Praeger, 1991).

2. Rost, *Leadership for the Twenty-First Century*, 143.

3. Rosabeth Moss Kanter, "What Inexperienced Leaders Get Wrong (Hint: Management)," *Harvard Business Review*, November 21, 2013.

4. Rost, *Leadership for the Twenty-First Century*.

5. Ronald A. Heifetz and Martin Linsky, *Leadership on the Line: Staying Alive through the Dangers of Leading* (Boston: Harvard Business School Press, 2002).

6. Rost, *Leadership for the Twenty-First Century*.

7. Rost, *Leadership for the Twenty-First Century*.

8. Heifetz and Linsky, *Leadership on the Line*.

9. Ronald A. Heifetz, *Leadership without Easy Answers* (Cambridge, MA: Belknap Press of Harvard University Press, 1994).

10. Jean Lau Chin, Joseph E. Trimble, and Joseph E. Garcia, eds., *Global and Culturally Diverse Leaders and Leadership: New Dimensions and Challenges for Business, Education and Society* (Bingley, UK: Emerald Publishing, 2018).

11. JoAnn Danelo Barbour et al., eds., *Leading in Complex Worlds* (San Francisco: Jossey-Bass, 2012).

12. Edgar H. Schein, *Humble Consulting: How to Provide Real Help Faster* (Oakland, CA: Berrett-Koehler Publishers, 2016).

13. James MacGregor Burns, *Leadership* (New York: Harper & Row, 1978).

14. Bernard M. Bass, "From Transactional to Transformational Leadership: Learning to Share the Vision," *Organizational Dynamics* 18, no. 3 (December 1990): 19–31, https://doi.org/10.1016/0090-2616(90)90061-S.

CHAPTER 4: TRANSFORMATIONAL, TRANSACTIONAL, AND CHARISMATIC APPROACHES

1. James MacGregor Burns, *Leadership* (New York: Harper & Row, 1978).

2. Burns, *Leadership*.

3. Bernard M. Bass, "From Transactional to Transformational Leadership: Learning to Share the Vision," *Organizational Dynamics* 18, no. 3 (December 1990): 21, https://doi.org/10.1016/0090-2616(90)90061-S.

4. Bass, "From Transactional to Transformational Leadership," 21.

5. Bass, "From Transactional to Transformational Leadership."

6. Bass, "From Transactional to Transformational Leadership."

7. Bass, "From Transactional to Transformational Leadership"; A. H. Maslow, "A Theory of Human Motivation," *Psychological Review* 50, no. 4 (July 1943): 370–96, https://doi.org/10.1037/h0054346.

8. Bass, "From Transactional to Transformational Leadership."

9. Nikolaos Dimitriadis and Alexandros Psychogios, *Neuroscience for Leaders: A Brain Adaptive Leadership Approach* (London: Kogan Page, 2016).

10. Dimitriadis and Psychogios, *Neuroscience for Leaders*, 60.

11. Simon Sinek, *Start with Why: How Great Leaders Inspire Everyone to Take Action* (New York: Penguin, 2011).

12. Dimitriadis and Psychogios, *Neuroscience for Leaders*.

13. Geert H. Hofstede, *Culture's Consequences: International Differences in Work-Related Values*, abridged ed., Cross-Cultural Research and Methodology Series (Beverly Hills: SAGE Publications, 1984).

14. David A. Nadler and Michael L. Tushman, "Beyond the Charismatic Leader: Leadership and Organizational Change," *California Management Review* 32, no. 2 (January 1990): 77–97, https://doi.org/10.2307/41166606.

15. James C. Collins, *Good to Great and the Social Sectors: A Monograph to Accompany* Good to Great: Why Some Companies Make the Leap…and Others Don't (Toronto: CNIB, 2005).

16. Nadler and Tushman, "Beyond the Charismatic Leader."

17. Michael Keeley, "The Trouble with Transformational Leadership: Toward a Federalist Ethic for Organizations," *Business Ethics Quarterly* 5, no. 1 (January 1995): 67–96, https://doi.org/10.2307/3857273; John E. Barbuto, "Taking the Charisma Out of Transformational Leadership," *Journal of Social Behavior and Personality* 12, no. 3 (1997): 689–97.

18. Jay Alden Conger, *The Charismatic Leader: Behind the Mystique of Exceptional Leadership*, The Jossey-Bass Management Series (San Francisco: Jossey-Bass, 1989).

19. Peter Guy Northouse, *Leadership: Theory and Practice*, 6th ed. (Thousand Oaks, CA: SAGE, 2013), 187.

20. Maslow, "A Theory of Human Motivation."

21. Maslow, "A Theory of Human Motivation."

22. Abraham H. Maslow, *Maslow on Management* (New York: Wiley, 1998).

23. Abraham H. Maslow, *The Farther Reaches of Human Nature* (New York: Arkana, 1993).

24. Maslow, *The Farther Reaches of Human Nature*, 228.

25. Maslow, *The Farther Reaches of Human Nature*, 228.

26. Frederic Herzberg, "The Motivation-Hygiene Concept and Problems of Manpower," *Personnel Administration* 27, no. 1 (1964): 3–7.

27. Frederick. Herzberg, *One More Time: How Do You Motivate Employees* (Boston: Harvard Business Review, 1968).

28. Northouse, *Leadership*.

29. Marshall Sashkin and Molly G. Sashkin, *Leadership That Matters: The Critical Factors for Making a Difference in People's Lives and Organizations' Success* (San Francisco: Berrett-Koehler, 2003).

30. Max Weber and Talcott Parsons, *The Theory of Social and Economic Organization*, trans. T. Parsons and A. M. Henderson (New York: Free Press, 1997).

31. Robert J. House, "A 1976 Theory of Charismatic Leadership. Working Paper Series 76-06" (Southern Illinois University Fourth Biennial Leadership Symposium, Carbondale Illinois: Toronto University, Oct. 1976).

32. John Antonakis and William L. Gardner, "Charisma: New Frontiers," *The Leadership Quarterly* 28, no. 4 (August 2017): 471–72, https://doi.org/10.1016/j.leaqua.2017.06.003.

33. Collins, *Good to Great and the Social Sectors*.

34. Burns, *Leadership*.

35. Jonathan Charteris-Black, *The Communication of Leadership: The Design of Leadership Style* (London: Routledge, 2006).

36. Charteris-Black, *Communication of Leadership*.

37. Antonakis and Gardner, "Charisma."

38. Conger, *The Charismatic Leader*.

39. Sashkin and Sashkin, *Leadership That Matters*, 69.

40. Sashkin and Sashkin, *Leadership That Matters*, 69.

41. Jerrold M. Post, "Narcissism and the Charismatic Leader-Follower Relationship," *Political Psychology* 7, no. 4 (December 1986): 675–87, https://doi.org/10.2307/3791208.

42. Burns, *Leadership*.

43. Deborah Barrett, *Leadership Communication*, 4th ed. (New York: McGraw-Hill Education, 2014).

CHAPTER 5: TRAITS, BEHAVIORS, AND SKILLS

1. Thomas Carlyle, *On Heroes, Hero-Worship, and the Heroic in History* (Boston: Houghton Mifflin, 1907), 18.

2. Ralph M. Stogdill, "Personal Factors Associated with Leadership: A Survey of the Literature," *The Journal of Psychology* 25, no. 1 (January 1948): 35–71, https://doi.org/10.1080/00223980.1948.9917362.

3. Stogdill, "Personal Factors," 66.

4. Shelley A. Kirkpatrick and Edwin A. Locke, "Leadership: Do Traits Matter?" *The Executive* 5, no. 2 (1991): 48–60.

5. James M. Kouzes and Barry Z. Posner, *The Leadership Challenge: How to Make Extraordinary Things Happen in Organizations*, 6th ed. (Hoboken, NJ: Leadership Challenge, 2017).

6. Daniel Goleman, *Emotional Intelligence* (New York: Bantam Books, 2005).

7. Robert L. Katz, "Skills of an Effective Administrator," *Harvard Business Review*, 1974.

8. Timothy A. Judge et al., "Personality and Leadership: A Qualitative and Quantitative Review," *Journal of Applied Psychology* 87, no. 4 (2002): 765–80, https://doi.org/10.1037/0021-9010.87.4.765.

9. Timothy A. Judge, Amy E. Colbert, and Remus Ilies, "Intelligence and Leadership: A Quantitative Review and Test of Theoretical Propositions," *Journal of Applied Psychology* 89, no. 3 (2004): 542–52, esp. 548, https://doi.org/10.1037/0021-9010.89.3.542.

10. Kouzes and Posner, *Leadership Challenge*.

11. Kouzes and Posner, *Leadership Challenge*.

12. Joseph C. Rost, *Leadership for the Twenty-First Century* (New York: Praeger, 1991).

13. Bernard M. Bass, "From Transactional to Transformational Leadership: Learning to Share the Vision," *Organizational Dynamics* 18, no. 3 (December 1990): 19–31, https://doi.org/10.1016/0090-2616(90)90061-S.

14. Karen Dill Bowerman and Montgomery Van Wart, *The Business of Leadership: An Introduction* (Armonk, NY: M. E. Sharpe, 2011).

15. Rost, *Leadership for the Twenty-First Century*.

16. Barbara Kellerman, *Followership: How Followers Are Creating Change and Changing Leaders* (Boston: Harvard Business School Press, 2008).

17. John P. Kotter, "What Leaders Really Do," *Harvard Business Review*, 1990.

18. Bowerman and Van Wart, *The Business of Leadership*.

19. Robert Blake and Jane S. Mouton, *The Managerial Grid: The Key to Leadership Excellence* (Houston: Gulf Publishing, 1964).

20. Timothy A. Judge, Ronald F. Piccolo, and Remus Ilies, "The Forgotten Ones? The Validity of Consideration and Initiating Structure in Leadership Research," *Journal of Applied Psychology* 89, no. 1 (2004): 36–51, https://doi.org/10.1037/0021-9010.89.1.36.

21. Robert Eugene Lefton and V. Ralph Buzzotta, *Leadership through People Skills* (New York: McGraw-Hill, 2004).

22. Lefton and Buzzotta, *Leadership through People Skills.*

23. Ralph K. White and Ronald Lippitt, *Autocracy and Democracy: An Experimental Inquiry* (Westport, CT: Greenwood Press, 1972).

24. Lefton and Buzzotta, *Leadership through People Skills.*

25. Lefton and Buzzotta, *Leadership through People Skills.*

26. Kouzes and Posner, *The Leadership Challenge.*

27. Kouzes and Posner, *The Leadership Challenge.*

28. Kouzes and Posner have developed many additional resources for each of the five practices.

29. Kouzes and Posner, *The Leadership Challenge.*

30. Kouzes and Posner, *The Leadership Challenge.*

31. Kouzes and Posner, *The Leadership Challenge.*

32. Katz, "Skills of an Effective Administrator."

33. Katz, "Skills of an Effective Administrator."

34. Katz, "Skills of an Effective Administrator."

35. Katz, "Skills of an Effective Administrator."

36. *McKinsey Report*, "Soft Skills for a Hard World" (blog), 2020, accessed August 10, 2020, https://www.mckinsey.com/business-functions/transformation/our-insights/five-fifty-the-changeable-organization.

37. D. Scott DeRue, "Adaptive Leadership Theory: Leading and Following as a Complex Adaptive Process," *Research in Organizational Behavior* 31 (January 2011): 125–50, https://doi.org/10.1016/j.riob.2011.09.007.

38. Kouzes and Posner, *The Leadership Challenge.*

CHAPTER 6: SITUATIONAL THEORIES AND LMX

1. Douglas McGregor, *The Human Side of Enterprise* (New York: McGraw-Hill, 1960).

2. Paul Hersey and Ken Blanchard, "Life Cycle Theory of Leadership," *Training and Development Journal* 23 (1969): 26–34.

3. Robert Blake and Jane S. Mouton, *The Managerial Grid: The Key to Leadership Excellence* (Houston: Gulf Publishing, 1964).

4. Robert Eugene Lefton and V. Ralph Buzzotta, *Leadership through People Skills* (New York: McGraw-Hill, 2004).

5. Hersey and Blanchard, "Life Cycle Theory of Leadership."

6. Edgar H. Schein, *Humble Inquiry: The Gentle Art of Asking Instead of Telling* (San Francisco: Berrett-Koehler, 2013).

7. Schein, *Humble Inquiry*.

8. Ronald A. Heifetz, Alexander Grashow, and Martin Linsky, *The Practice of Adaptive Leadership: Tools and Tactics for Changing Your Organization and the World* (Boston: Harvard Business Press, 2009).

9. Dan R. Ebener, *Blessings for Leaders: Leadership Wisdom from the Beatitudes* (Collegeville, MN: Liturgical Press, 2012).

10. Schein, *Humble Inquiry*.

11. Joseph C. Rost, *Leadership for the Twenty-First Century* (New York: Praeger, 1991).

12. Robert J. House and Terrence R. Mitchell, "Path-Goal Theory of Leadership," *Contemporary Business* 3 (1974): 81–98.

13. Robert J. House, "A Path Goal Theory of Leader Effectiveness," *Administrative Science Quarterly* 16, no. 3 (September 1971): 321, https://doi.org/10.2307/2391905.

14. House and Mitchell, "Path-Goal Theory of Leadership."

15. House and Mitchell, "Path-Goal Theory of Leadership."

16. House and Mitchell, "Path-Goal Theory of Leadership."

17. Robert J. House, "Path-Goal Theory of Leadership: Lessons, Legacy, and a Reformulated Theory," *The Leadership Quarterly* 7, no. 3 (September 1996): 323–52, https://doi.org/10.1016/S1048-9843(96)90024-7.

18. Karen Dill Bowerman and Montgomery Van Wart, *The Business of Leadership: An Introduction* (Armonk, NY: M. E. Sharpe, 2011).

19. G. Graen and J. Cashman, "A Role Making Model of Leadership in Formal Organizations: A Developmental Approach," in *Leadership Frontiers*, ed. J. G. Hunt and L. L. Larson (Kent, OH: Kent State University Press, 1975), 143–65.

20. Graen and Cashman, "Role Making Model of Leadership."

21. George B. Graen and Mary Uhl-Bien, "Relationship-Based Approach to Leadership: Development of Leader-Member Exchange (LMX) Theory of Leadership over 25 Years: Applying a Multi-level Multi-domain Perspective," *Leadership Quarterly* 6, no. 2 (1995): 219–47.

22. Graen and Uhl-Bien, "Relationship-Based Approach."

23. Bowerman and Van Wart, *The Business of Leadership*.

24. Afsaneh Nahavandi, *The Art and Science of Leadership*, 7th ed. (Boston: Pearson, 2015).

25. Bowerman and Van Wart, *The Business of Leadership*.

26. Bernard M. Bass, "From Transactional to Transformational Leadership: Learning to Share the Vision," *Organizational Dynamics* 18, no. 3 (Winter 1990): 21, https://doi.org/10.1016/0090-2616(90)90061-S.

27. Dale Carnegie, *How to Win Friends and Influence People: The First—and Still the Best—Book of Its Kind—to Lead You to Success* (New York: Simon and Schuster, 1981).

PART III: BEST PRACTICES IN LEADERSHIP

INTRODUCTION

1. Dan R. Ebener, *Pastoral Leadership: Best Practices for Church Leaders* (Mahwah, NJ: Paulist Press, 2018).

2. John Wooden and Steve Jamison, *Wooden on Leadership* (New York: McGraw-Hill, 2005).

3. Patrick Lencioni, *The Five Dysfunctions of a Team: A Leadership Fable* (San Francisco: Jossey-Bass, 2002).

4. Daniel Goleman, *Emotional Intelligence* (New York: Bantam Books, 2005).

5. Edgar H. Schein, *Humble Inquiry: The Gentle Art of Asking Instead of Telling* (San Francisco: Berrett-Koehler, 2013).

6. William Isaacs, *Dialogue and the Art of Thinking Together: A Pioneering Approach to Communicating in Business and in Life* (New York: Currency, 1999).

7. Randy L. Richards, *Conflict and Collaboration: The Search for the Integrative Space* (Rock Island, IL: Richards, 2017).

8. Karen A. Jehn, "A Multimethod Examination of the Benefits and Detriments of Intragroup Conflict," *Administrative Science Quarterly* 40, no. 2 (June 1995): 256, https://doi.org/10.2307/2393638.

9. Dan R. Ebener and Frederick L. Smith, *Strategic Planning: An Interactive Process for Leaders* (Mahwah, NJ: Paulist Press, 2015).

CHAPTER 7: EMOTIONAL SKILLS

1. Daniel Goleman, *Emotional Intelligence* (New York: Bantam Books, 2005).

2. Goleman, *Emotional Intelligence*.

3. Sharon Begley, *How a New Science Reveals Our Extraordinary Potential to Transform Ourselves* (New York: Ballantine Books, 2007).

4. Goleman, *Emotional Intelligence*.

5. Goleman, *Emotional Intelligence*.

6. Seth Gillihan, *Retrain Your Brain: Cognitive Behavioral Therapy in 7 Weeks* (Berkeley, CA: Althea Press, 2016).

7. Goleman, *Emotional Intelligence*.

8. James C. Collins, *Good to Great and the Social Sectors: A Monograph to Accompany* Good to Great: Why Some Companies Make the Leap...and Others Don't (Toronto: CNIB, 2005).

9. Matthias Birk, "What Meditation Can Do for Your Leadership," *Harvard Business Review*, 2019.

10. Birk, "What Meditation Can Do."

11. Ronald A. Heifetz and Martin Linsky, *Leadership on the Line: Staying Alive through the Dangers of Leading* (Boston: Harvard Business School Press, 2002).

12. Begley, *How a New Science Reveals Our Extraordinary Potential to Transform Ourselves*.

13. Begley, *How a New Science Reveals Our Extraordinary Potential to Transform Ourselves*.

14. Joseph Chilton Pearce, *The Biology of Transcendence: A Blueprint of the Human Spirit* (Rochester, VT: Park Street Press, 2004).

15. Begley, *How a New Science Reveals Our Extraordinary Potential to Transform Ourselves*.

16. Begley, *How a New Science Reveals Our Extraordinary Potential to Transform Ourselves*.

17. Richard J. Davidson and Sharon Begley, *The Emotional Life of Your Brain: How Its Unique Patterns Affect the Way You Think, Feel, and Live—and How You Can Change Them* (New York: Plume, 2013).

18. Birk, "What Meditation Can Do for Your Leadership."

19. Mark Goulston, *Just Listen: Discover the Secret to Getting Through to Absolutely Anyone* (New York: American Management Association, 2010).

20. Goleman, *Emotional Intelligence*.

21. Daniel Friedland, *Leading Well from Within: A Neuroscience and Mindfulness-Based Framework for Conscious Leadership* (San Diego: SuperSmartHealth, 2016).

22. Begley, *How a New Science Reveals Our Extraordinary Potential to Transform Ourselves*.

23. Nikolaos Dimitriadis and Alexandros Psychogios, *Neuroscience for Leaders: A Brain Adaptive Leadership Approach* (London: Kogan Page, 2016).

24. Goleman, *Emotional Intelligence*.

25. Goleman, *Emotional Intelligence*.

26. Goleman, *Emotional Intelligence*; Travis Bradberry and Jean Greaves, *Emotional Intelligence 2.0* (San Diego: TalentSmart, 2009).

27. David Bohm and Lee Nichol, *On Dialogue* (New York: Routledge, 2004).

28. Viktor Emil Frankl, *Man's Search for Meaning* (Boston: Beacon Press, 2006).

29. Dimitriadis and Psychogios, *Neuroscience for Leaders*.

30. Goleman, *Emotional Intelligence*.

31. Bradberry and Greaves, *Emotional Intelligence 2.0*.

32. Goleman, *Emotional Intelligence*.

33. David Rock, *Your Brain at Work: Strategies for Overcoming Distraction, Regaining Focus, and Working Smarter All Day Long* (New York: Harper Business, 2009).

34. Davidson and Begley, *Emotional Life of Your Brain*.

35. Rock, *Your Brain at Work*.

36. Gillihan, *Retrain Your Brain*.

37. Bradberry and Greaves, *Emotional Intelligence 2.0*.

38. Goleman, *Emotional Intelligence*.

39. Michael P. Ventura, *Applied Empathy: The New Language of Leadership* (New York: Touchstone, 2018).

40. Brené Brown, *Dare to Lead: Brave Work, Tough Conversations, Whole Hearts* (New York: Random House, 2018).

41. Davidson and Begley, *Emotional Life of Your Brain.*

42. Bradberry and Greaves, *Emotional Intelligence 2.0.*

43. Goleman, *Emotional Intelligence.*

44. Begley, *How a New Science Reveals Our Extraordinary Potential to Transform Ourselves.*

45. Davidson and Begley, *Emotional Life of Your Brain.*

46. Ventura, *Applied Empathy.*

47. Begley, *How a New Science Reveals Our Extraordinary Potential to Transform Ourselves.*

48. Bradberry and Greaves, *Emotional Intelligence 2.0.*

49. Dimitriadis and Psychogios, *Neuroscience for Leaders.*

CHAPTER 8: DIALOGICAL SKILLS

1. William Isaacs, *Dialogue and the Art of Thinking Together: A Pioneering Approach to Communicating in Business and in Life* (New York: Currency, 1999).

2. Joseph C. Rost, *Leadership for the Twenty-First Century* (New York: Praeger, 1991).

3. Don Cohen and Laurence Prusak, *In Good Company: How Social Capital Makes Organizations Work* (Boston: Harvard Business School Press, 2001).

4. Patrick Lencioni, *The Five Dysfunctions of a Team: A Leadership Fable* (San Francisco: Jossey-Bass, 2002).

5. Lencioni, *Five Dysfunctions of a Team*, 195.

6. Roger Fisher, William Ury, and Bruce Patton, *Getting to Yes: Negotiating an Agreement without Giving In*, 2nd ed. (London: Random House Business Books, 1999).

7. Lencioni, *Five Dysfunctions of a Team.*

8. Chip Conley, *Wisdom@work: The Making of a Modern Elder* (New York: Currency, 2018).

9. Edgar H. Schein, *Humble Inquiry: The Gentle Art of Asking Instead of Telling* (San Francisco: Berrett-Koehler, 2013).

10. Schein, *Humble Inquiry.*

11. Schein, *Humble Inquiry.*

12. Schein, *Humble Inquiry.*

13. Ronald A. Heifetz and Martin Linsky, *Leadership on the Line: Staying Alive through the Dangers of Leading* (Boston: Harvard Business School Press, 2002).

14. Mark Goulston, *Just Listen: Discover the Secret to Getting Through to Absolutely Anyone* (New York: American Management Association, 2010).

15. Michael J. Marquardt, *Leading with Questions: How Leaders Find the Right Solutions by Knowing What to Ask*, rev. and updated ed. (San Francisco: Jossey-Bass, 2014).

16. Marquardt, *Leading with Questions.*

17. Schein, *Humble Inquiry*.

18. Schein, *Humble Inquiry*.

19. Dan R. Ebener, *Blessings for Leaders: Leadership Wisdom from the Beatitudes* (Collegeville, MN: Liturgical Press, 2012).

20. David Bohm and Lee Nichol, *On Dialogue* (New York: Routledge, 2004).

21. Marquardt, *Leading with Questions*.

22. Daniel Coyle, *Culture Power* (n.p.: Random House Business, 2016).

23. Conley, *Wisdom@work*, 85.

24. Conley, *Wisdom@work*, 85.

25. Schein, *Humble Inquiry*.

26. Nikolaos Dimitriadis and Alexandros Psychogios, *Neuroscience for Leaders: A Brain Adaptive Leadership Approach* (London: Kogan Page, 2016).

27. Isaacs, *Dialogue and the Art of Thinking Together*.

28. James M. Kouzes and Barry Z. Posner, *The Truth about Leadership: The No-Fads, Heart-of-the-Matter Facts You Need to Know* (San Francisco: Jossey-Bass, 2010).

29. Isaacs, *Dialogue and the Art of Thinking Together*.

30. Janice Marturano, *Finding the Space to Lead: A Practical Guide to Mindful Leadership* (London: Bloomsbury, 2015).

31. Isaacs, *Dialogue and the Art of Thinking Together*.

32. Isaacs, *Dialogue and the Art of Thinking Together*.

33. Isaacs, *Dialogue and the Art of Thinking Together*.

34. Dimitriadis and Psychogios, *Neuroscience for Leaders*.

35. Marturano, *Finding the Space to Lead*.

36. Dalai Lama, *How to Practice: The Way to a Meaningful Life*, trans. Jeffrey Hopkins (New York: Atria Books, 2003).

37. Claus Otto Scharmer and Katrin Kaufer, *Leading from the Emerging Future: From Ego-System to Eco-System Economies* (San Francisco: Berrett-Koehler Publishers, 2013).

38. Isaacs, *Dialogue and the Art of Thinking Together*.

39. Rost, *Leadership for the Twenty-First Century*.

CHAPTER 9: CONFLICT SKILLS

1. Kenneth W. Thomas, "Conflict and Negotiation Processes in Organizations," in *Handbook of Industrial and Organizational Psychology*, ed. M. D. Dunnette and L. M. Hough (Palo Alto, CA: Consulting Psychologists Press, 1992), 651–717.

2. Janice Marturano, *Finding the Space to Lead: A Practical Guide to Mindful Leadership* (London: Bloomsbury, 2015).

3. Karen A. Jehn, "A Multimethod Examination of the Benefits and Detriments of Intragroup Conflict," *Administrative Science Quarterly* 40, no. 2 (June 1995), https://doi.org/10.2307/2393638; K. A. Jehn and E. A. Mannix, "The Dynamic Nature of Conflict: A Longitudinal Study of Intragroup Conflict and Group Performance," *Academy of Management Journal* 44, no. 2 (April 1, 2001): 238–51.

4. Irving L. Janis, "Groupthink," *Psychology Today* 5, no. 6 (1971): 43–46, 74–76.

5. Jehn, "A Multimethod Examination of the Benefits and Detriments of Intragroup Conflict"; A. C. Amason, "Distinguishing the Effects of Functional and Dysfunctional Conflict on Strategic Decision Making: Resolving a Paradox for Top Management Teams," *Academy of Management Journal* 39, no. 1 (February 1, 1996): 123–48.

6. Roger Fisher, William Ury, and Bruce Patton, *Getting to Yes: Negotiating an Agreement without Giving In*, 2nd ed. (London: Random House Business Books, 1999).

7. Jehn, "Multimethod Examination of the Benefits and Detriments of Intragroup Conflict"; Amason, "Distinguishing the Effects of Functional and Dysfunctional Conflict on Strategic Decision Making."

8. Friedrich Glasl, *Konfliktmanagement: ein Handbuch für Führungskräfte, Beraterinnen und Berater*, aktualisierte Auflage (Bern: Haupt Verlag, 2013), 11.

9. Glasl, *Konfliktmanagement*.

10. Thomas, "Conflict and Negotiation Processes in Organizations."

11. Thomas, "Conflict and Negotiation Processes in Organizations."

12. Edgar H. Schein, *Humble Inquiry: The Gentle Art of Asking Instead of Telling* (San Francisco: Berrett-Koehler, 2013).

13. It is important to distinguish conflict avoidance from conflict prevention. Preventing a conflict from escalating from task conflict to relational conflict is healthy. Avoiding the conflict altogether can be destructive to both the task and the relationship. It tends to escalate those inevitable disagreements called task conflict into relationship conflict.

14. Thomas, "Conflict and Negotiation Processes in Organizations."

15. When we teach this model, we usually suggest that there is space within the Q4 quadrant and that we might move in the direction of Q1 or Q3—without crossing over the line into that quadrant. For example, you might be at the Christmas party when someone initiates a discussion about some conflict brewing. It might be appropriate at that time to move toward a less assertive approach (Q3) but to make it clear that the conflict will be addressed at another time. This means that you do not abandon the Q4 quadrant, but you move around it, based on the situation.

16. Fisher, Ury, and Patton, *Getting to Yes*.

17. Fisher, Ury, and Patton, *Getting to Yes*.

18. Thomas, "Conflict and Negotiation Processes in Organizations."

19. Thomas, "Conflict and Negotiation Processes in Organizations."

20. Daniel Goleman, *Emotional Intelligence* (New York: Bantam Books, 2005).

21. David Rock, *Your Brain at Work: Strategies for Overcoming Distraction, Regaining Focus, and Working Smarter All Day Long* (New York: Harper Business, 2009).

22. Nikolaos Dimitriadis and Alexandros Psychogios, *Neuroscience for Leaders: A Brain Adaptive Leadership Approach* (London: Kogan Page, 2016).

23. Goleman, *Emotional Intelligence*.

24. Goleman, *Emotional Intelligence*.

25. Robert Eugene Lefton and V. Ralph Buzzotta, *Leadership through People Skills* (New York: McGraw-Hill, 2004).

26. Goleman, *Emotional Intelligence*.

27. Rock, *Your Brain at Work*.

28. Goleman, *Emotional Intelligence*.

29. Randy L. Richards, *Conflict and Collaboration: The Search for the Integrative Space* (Rock Island, IL: Richards, 2017).

30. Fisher, Ury, and Patton, *Getting to Yes*.

31. Fisher, Ury, and Patton, *Getting to Yes*.

32. Thomas, "Conflict and Negotiation Processes in Organizations."

33. Richards, *Conflict and Collaboration*.

34. Richards, *Conflict and Collaboration*.

35. Fisher, Ury, and Patton, *Getting to Yes*.

36. Roger Fisher and Scott Brown, *Getting Together: Building Relationships as We Negotiate* (New York: Penguin, 1989).

CHAPTER 10: STRATEGIC SKILLS

1. Dan R. Ebener and Frederick L. Smith, *Strategic Planning: An Interactive Process for Leaders* (Mahwah, NJ: Paulist Press, 2015).

2. Ebener and Smith, *Strategic Planning*.

3. Ebener and Smith, *Strategic Planning*.

4. Ebener and Smith, *Strategic Planning*.

5. Irving L. Janis, "Groupthink," *Psychology Today* 5, no. 6 (1971): 43–46, 74–76.

6. Ebener and Smith, *Strategic Planning*.

7. John M. Bryson, *Strategic Planning for Public and Nonprofit Organizations: A Guide to Strengthening and Sustaining Organizational Achievement* (San Francisco: Jossey-Bass, 2004).

8. Ebener and Smith, *Strategic Planning*.

9. Kenneth H. Blanchard, Michael J. O'Connor, and Jim Ballard, *Managing by Values: How to Put Your Values into Action for Extraordinary Results* (San Francisco: Berrett-Koehler, 2003).

10. Michael Allison and Jude Kaye, *Strategic Planning for Nonprofit Organizations: A Practical Guide and Workbook*, 2nd ed. (Hoboken, NJ: Wiley, 2005).

11. James C. Collins and Jerry I. Porras, "CMR Classics: Organizational Vision and Visionary Organizations," *California Management Review* 50, no. 2 (January 2008): 117–37, https://doi.org/10.2307/41166438.

12. Collins and Porras, "CMR Classics."

13. Allison and Kaye, *Strategic Planning for Nonprofit Organizations*.

14. Collins and Porras, "CMR Classics."

15. Collins and Porras, "CMR Classics."

16. Bryson, *Strategic Planning for Public and Nonprofit Organizations*.

17. For further information please look at Dan R. Ebener and Frederick L. Smith, *Strategic Planning: An Interactive Process for Leaders* (Mahwah, NJ: Paulist Press, 2015).

18. Bryson, *Strategic Planning for Public and Nonprofit Organizations*.

19. John P. Kotter, *A Sense of Urgency* (Boston: Harvard Business Press, 2008).

20. Ronald A. Heifetz and Martin Linsky, *Leadership on the Line: Staying Alive through the Dangers of Leading* (Boston: Harvard Business School Press, 2002).

21. Ebener and Smith, *Strategic Planning*.

22. Ebener and Smith, *Strategic Planning*.

23. Ebener and Smith, *Strategic Planning*.

24. Ebener and Smith, *Strategic Planning*.

25. Burt Nanus, *Leading the Way to Organization Renewal*, Management Master Series (Portland, OR: Productivity Press, 1996).

26. James C. Collins and Jerry I. Porras, *Built to Last: Successful Habits of Visionary Companies* (New York: Harper Business, 2004).

27. Bryson, *Strategic Planning for Public and Nonprofit Organizations*.

28. Ebener and Smith, *Strategic Planning*.

29. This is a principle in community organizing.

30. Ebener and Smith, *Strategic Planning*.

31. Schein, *Humble Inquiry*.

32. John P. Lotter, *Leading Change* (Boston: Harvard Business School Press, 1996).

33. Ebener and Smith, *Strategic Planning*.

34. Scott K. Edinger and Laurie Sain, *The Hidden Leader: Discover and Develop Greatness within Your Company* (New York: AMACOM, 2015).

35. Allan R. Cohen and David L. Bradford, *Influence without Authority*, 2nd ed. (Hoboken, NJ: Wiley, 2005).

CONCLUSION: LEADING WITH AND LEADING WITHOUT AUTHORITY

1. For example, Pope Francis.

2. Scott K. Edinger and Laurie Sain, *The Hidden Leader: Discover and Develop Greatness within Your Company* (New York: AMACOM, 2015).

3. Warren Bennis and Burt Nanus, *The Strategies for Taking Charge* (New York: Harper & Row, 1985).

4. Ronald A. Heifetz and Martin Linsky, *Leadership on the Line: Staying Alive through the Dangers of Leading* (Boston: Harvard Business School Press, 2002).

5. Ronald A. Heifetz, *Leadership without Easy Answers* (Cambridge, MA: Belknap Press of Harvard University Press, 1994).

6. Allan R. Cohen and David L. Bradford, *Influence without Authority*, 2nd ed. (Hoboken, NJ: Wiley, 2005).

GLOSSARY

Adaptive challenges: Issues for which there are no easy answers or technical solutions

Adaptive leadership: Leadership that addresses adaptive challenges (see above)

Amygdala: The front sections of the limbic system responsible for fear and anger responses

Assertive: Expressing yourself with neither passivity nor hostility

Attunement: From Old English for "to bring into harmony," to tune into the emotions of another

Authority: From Latin for "originator," the formal power that comes from a position

Behaviors: Pattern of actions taken by a person, what they do

Brain: The physical center of the emotional, intellectual, and nervous system

Categorical imperative: Unconditional moral rule or law without need of further support

Character: From Greek for "distinctive mark," the fruits of practicing virtue

Charisma: From Greek for "gift from God," or in English, attraction toward another

Closed question: Question that can be answered with one specific answer, e.g., yes or no

Coercive power: Ability to fire, discipline, and make decisions that force others to comply

Collaboration: From Latin for "work together," integrating the needs and interests of both parties

Concept mapping: Activity where group is asked to draw a picture of an abstract concept

Consensus: From Latin for "agreement," one that everyone can live with

Consent agenda: Agreement to approve all written reports in one motion

Conversation Cafes: Activity that allows small groups to contribute to multiple conversations

Culture: From Latin for "to cultivate," values, customs, and beliefs of an organization or a country

Debate: From Latin for "to batter," a discussion where both parties intend to compete and win

Deflect: To respond to a question by asking others what they think

Delegation: From Latin for "to commission," to pass a responsibility (with support and feedback)

Deontological: From Greek for "necessary," the focus is on moral duties, also known as duty ethics

Dialogue: From Greek for "to gather together," or "to speak through," a conversation

Dirty hands: An ethical question of whether to violate morality in order to reach a moral goal

Emotional intelligence: Self-awareness, self-control, social awareness, and social guidance

Emotional quotient (EQ): A measure of emotional intelligence (EI)

Emotions: From Latin for "to move," your physiological reaction to an event

Empathy: From Greek for "feeling" or "passion," the ability to share the emotions of another

Engagement: French for "to pledge," an emotional attachment to a person or organization

Ethics: From Greek for "custom" or "habits," the study of moral principles, norms, and values

Expert power: Power to influence others stemming from personal expertise

Extrinsic motivation: From Latin for "outward," rewards or punishments

Followers: Those who are actively involved in leadership, often being trained for leadership

Generative dialogue: Open conversation that keeps focus on the emerging consensus

Generative listening: Listening with open mind, open heart, and open will

Humble inquiry: A process of asking questions with humility, empathy, and curiosity

Humility: From Greek for "earthly," being fully aware of human strengths and weaknesses

Inquiry: From Latin for "to seek within," the process of asking questions

Inspiration: From Latin for "to breathe within," to motivate the "spirit"

Intrinsic motivation: From Latin for "inward," to be moved by the mind, spirit, or heart

Laisseiz-faire: French for "leave alone"; "let do"

Leader-member exchange (LMX): Focus is on in-groups and out-groups

Leadership: Voluntary, interactive influence process that intends adaptive change

Leading question: Question that poses the suggested answer within the question

Legitimate authority: Power that authorizes a person with positional authority

Limbic system: The emotional center of the brain

Loaded question: Question that assumes the worst in the person being questioned

Management: Positional authority with administrative responsibility for certain operations

Micromanagement: Controlling the actions of workers down to every little detail

Mind: Conscious awareness that interprets and can control what is happening in the brain

Mindfulness: Being fully alert, conscious, or aware, living fully in the present moment

Mission: Your bottom-line purpose, your reason for being, the social benefit you provide

Morality: Set of principles defining what is right or wrong in a certain culture

Narcissism: From Greek for "self-love," or in English, arrogance

Neuroplasticity: The ability of the brain to change and grow

Normative ethics: Type of ethics answering the question, How should things be?

Open question: Question that opens the other person to discussing whatever they want

Organizational citizenship: A person's voluntary commitment to an organization

Path-goal theory: An industrial theory suggesting supervisory style for various situations

Power: From Latin for "to be able," the ability to act

Proprioception: From Latin for "own reception," includes ability to think about your thoughts

Prosocial behavior: Positive actions that build social capital (see below)

Pseudo: From Greek for "false"

Quid pro quo: Latin phrase meaning "something for something"

Receptivity: From Latin for "to receive," the level of openness, readiness to listen

Referent power: Ability to influence based on character and reputation

Reflective probe: Calling an emotion by name during a dialogue

Relationship conflict: Disagreements that escalate into people problems

Relationship of leadership: The trust, commitment, and cohesion within the team

Respect: From Latin for "to look again," to recognize the dignity of the other person

Self-awareness: Ability to be aware of your own emotions

Self-control: Ability to guide your own behavior, especially during an emotional episode

Servant leadership: Leadership based on a motivation first to serve and then to lead

Shared vision: Common goal or vision that is cocreated by the whole team

Situational theories: Based on level of cooperation and direction needed per situation

Social awareness: Ability to identify with the emotions of others

Social capital: The measure of relationships on a team, including trust, loyalty, and cohesion

Social intelligence: Social awareness plus social skills (two parts of emotional intelligence)

Social skills: Ability to handle gracefully the emotions of others

Strategic: From Greek for "general's view of the battlefield," a comprehensive overview

Strategic issue: Critical, comprehensive, changeable problem facing an organization

Strategic planning: Process of establishing strategic goals, strategies, and action steps

Strategy: Possible solution to a strategic issue

Structure: From Latin for "to build," arrangement of systems, departments, or divisions

Subordinate: From Latin for "inferior rank," or "less than ordinary," those of a lower position

Summaries: Shortened version of what the other person is saying

SWOT: Strengths and Weaknesses (internal); Opportunities and Threats (external)

Synergy: Team cohesion resulting in the whole being greater than the sum of the parts

Task conflict: Disagreement about the task itself, e.g., the solution to a problem

Task of leadership: The strategy, the goal, or the intended change

Technical solution: Applying what is already known to fix a problem

Teleological: From Greek for "the ends," focus is on consequences or results (not intentions)

Traits: Characteristics or qualities that describes a person

Transactional: Based on extrinsic motivators such as transactions

Transformational: Based on intrinsic motivators such as inspiration

Virtue: From Latin for "moral perfection," a trait that helps achieve lasting joy or happiness

Vision: From Latin for "to see," the picture of success, the future direction of your organization

Voluntary: From Latin for "will," acting from one's free will, not from coercion

Wisdom: From Greek for knowledge plus learning plus experience

REFERENCES

Allison, Michael, and Jude Kaye. *Strategic Planning for Nonprofit Organizations: A Practical Guide and Workbook*. 2nd ed. Hoboken, NJ: Wiley, 2005.

Amason, A. C. "Distinguishing the Effects of Functional and Dysfunctional Conflict on Strategic Decision Making: Resolving a Paradox for Top Management Teams." *Academy of Management Journal* 39, no. 1 (February 1, 1996): 123–48.

Antonakis, John, and William L. Gardner. "Charisma: New Frontiers." *The Leadership Quarterly* 28, no. 4 (August 2017): 471–72. https://doi.org/10.1016/j.leaqua.2017.06.003.

Barach, Jeffrey A., and D. Reed Eckhardt. *Leadership and the Job of the Executive*. Westport, CT: Quorum Books, 1996.

Barbour, JoAnn Danelo, Gloria Burgess, Lena Lid Falkman, and Robert M. McManus, eds. *Leading in Complex Worlds: Building Leadership Bridges*. San Francisco: Jossey-Bass, 2012.

Barbuto, John E. "Taking the Charisma Out of Transformational Leadership." *Journal of Social Behavior and Personality* 12, no. 3 (1997): 689–97.

Barrett, Deborah. *Leadership Communication*. 4th ed. New York: McGraw-Hill Education, 2014.

Bass, Bernard M. "From Transactional to Transformational Leadership: Learning to Share the Vision." *Organizational Dynamics* 18, no. 3 (December 1990): 19–31. https://doi.org/10.1016/0090-2616(90)90061-S.

Bass, Bernard M., and Ralph M. Stogdill. *Bass & Stogdill's Handbook of Leadership: Theory, Research, and Managerial Applications*. 3rd ed. New York: Free Press; London: Collier Macmillan, 1990.

Beer, Michael, Magnus Finnstrom, and Derek Schrader. "Why Leadership Training Fails—and What to Do About It." *Harvard Business Review*, October 2016, 50–57.

Begley, Sharon. *Train Your Mind, Change Your Brain: How a New Science Reveals Our Extraordinary Potential to Transform Ourselves*. New York: Ballantine Books, 2007.

Bennis, Warren, and Burt Nanus. *The Strategies for Taking Charge*. New York: Harper & Row, 1985.

Birk, Mathias. "What Meditation Can Do for Your Leadership." *Harvard Business Review*, 2019.

Blake, Robert, and Jane S. Mouton. *The Managerial Grid: The Key to Leadership Excellence*. Houston: Gulf Publishing Company, 1964.

Blanchard, Kenneth H, Michael J. O'Connor, and Jim Ballard. *Managing by Values: How to Put Your Values into Action for Extraordinary Results*. San Francisco: Berrett-Koehler, 2003.

Bohm, David, and Lee Nichol. *On Dialogue*. Routledge Classics. London: Routledge, 2004.

Bolman, Lee G., and Terrence E. Deal. *Reframing Organizations: Artistry, Choice, and Leadership*. The Jossey-Bass Management Series. San Francisco: Jossey-Bass, 1991.

Bowerman, Karen Diller, and Montgomery Van Wart. *The Business of Leadership: An Introduction*. Armonk, NY: M.E. Sharpe, 2011.

Bowie, Norman E. "Expanding the Horizons of Leadership." In *The Quest for Moral Leaders: Essays on Leadership Ethics*, 144–60. Northampton, MA: Edward Elgar Publishing, 2005.

Bradberry, Travis, and Jean Greaves. *Emotional Intelligence 2.0*. San Diego: TalentSmart, 2009.

Brown, Brené. *Dare to Lead: Brave Work, Tough Conversations, Whole Hearts*. New York: Random House, 2018.

Brown, Kirk Warren, and Richard M. Ryan. "The Benefits of Being Present: Mindfulness and Its Role in Psychological Well-Being." *Journal of Personality and Social Psychology* 84, no. 4 (2003): 822–48. https://doi.org/10.1037/0022-3514.84.4.822.

Bryson, John M. *Strategic Planning for Public and Nonprofit Organizations: A Guide to Strengthening and Sustaining Organizational Achievement*. San Francisco: Jossey-Bass, 2004.

Burns, James MacGregor. *Leadership*. New York: Harper & Row, 1978.

Carlyle, Thomas. *On Heroes, Hero-Worship, and the Heroic in History*. Boston: Houghton Mifflin, 1907.

Carnegie, Dale. *How to Win Friends and Influence People: The First—and Still the Best—Book of Its Kind to Lead You to Success*. New York: Simon and Schuster, 1981.

Charteris-Black, Jonathan. *The Communication of Leadership: The Design of Leadership Style*. London: Routledge, 2006. https://doi.org/10.4324/9780203968291.

Chin, Jean Lau, Joseph E. Trimble, and Joseph E. Garcia, eds. *Global and Culturally Diverse Leaders and Leadership: New Dimensions and Challenges for Business, Education and Society*. Building Leadership Bridges. Bingley, UK: Emerald Publishing, 2018.

Ciulla, Joanne B. "Leadership Ethics." In *International Encyclopedia of Ethics*, 1–7. Oxford, UK: John Wiley & Sons, Ltd, 2017. https://doi.org/10.1002/9781444367072.wbiee370.pub2.

———. "Leadership Ethics: Mapping the Territory." *Business Ethics Quarterly* 5, no. 1 (January 1995): 5–28. https://doi.org/10.2307/3857269.

Ciulla, Joanne B., David Knights, Chris Mabey, and Leah Tomkins. "Guest Editors' Introduction: Philosophical Contributions to Leadership Ethics." *Business Ethics Quarterly* 28, no. 1 (2018): 1–14. https://doi.org/10.1017/beq.2017.48.

Coady, C. A. J. "The Problem of Dirty Hands." In *The Stanford Encyclopedia of Philosophy*, edited by Edward N. Zalta. Metaphysics Research Lab, Stanford University, 2018. https://plato.stanford.edu/archives/fall2018/entries/dirty-hands/.

Cohen, Allan R., and David L. Bradford. *Influence without Authority*. 2nd ed. Hoboken, NJ: Wiley, 2005.

Cohen, Don, and Laurence Prusak. *In Good Company: How Social Capital Makes Organizations Work*. Boston: Harvard Business School Press, c2001, n.d.

Collins, James C. *Good to Great and the Social Sectors: A Monograph to Accompany Good to Great: Why Some Companies Make the Leap...and Others Don't*. Toronto: CNIB, 2005.

Collins, James C., and Jerry I. Porras. *Built to Last: Successful Habits of Visionary Companies*. New York: Harper Business, 2004.

———. "CMR Classics: Organizational Vision and Visionary Organizations." *California Management Review* 50, no. 2 (January 2008): 117–37. https://doi.org/10.2307/41166438.

Conger, Jay Alden. *The Charismatic Leader: Behind the Mystique of Exceptional Leadership*. The Jossey-Bass Management Series. San Francisco: Jossey-Bass Publishers, 1989.

Conley, Chip. *Wisdom@work: The Making of a Modern Elder*. New York: Currency, 2018.

Coyle, Daniel. *Culture Power*. N.p.: Random House Business, 2016.

Craig, Nick. *Leading from Purpose*. New York: Hachette Books, 2018.

Davidson, Richard J., and Sharon Begley. *The Emotional Life of Your Brain: How Its Unique Patterns Affect the Way You Think, Feel, and Live—and How You Can Change Them*. New York: Plume, 2013.

Deal, Terrence E., and Allan A. Kennedy. *Corporate Cultures: The Rites and Rituals of Corporate Life*. Cambridge, MA: Perseus, 2000.

Deci, Edward L. *Intrinsic Motivation*. Boston: Springer US, 1975. https://doi.org/10.1007/978-1-4613-4446-9.

Deci, Edward L., and Richard M. Ryan. "The Support of Autonomy and the Control of Behavior." *Journal of Personality and Social Psychology* 53, no. 6 (1987): 1024–37. https://doi.org/10.1037/0022-3514.53.6.1024.

———. "The 'What' and 'Why' of Goal Pursuits: Human Needs and the Self-Determination of Behavior." *Psychological Inquiry* 11, no. 4 (October 2000): 227–68. https://doi.org/10.1207/S15327965PLI1104_01.

DeRue, D. Scott. "Adaptive Leadership Theory: Leading and Following as a Complex Adaptive Process." *Research in Organizational Behavior* 31 (January 2011): 125–50. https://doi.org/10.1016/j.riob.2011.09.007.

DeRue, D. Scott, and Susan J. Ashford. "Who Will Lead and Who Will Follow? A Social Process of Leadership Identity Construction in Organizations." *The Academy of Management Review* 35, no. 4 (2010): 627–47.

Dimitriadis, Nikolaos, and Alexandros Psychogios. *Neuroscience for Leaders: A Brain Adaptive Leadership Approach.* London: Kogan Page, 2016.

Drucker, Peter F. *Management: Tasks, Responsibilities, Practices.* Harper Colophon Books, CN/1207. New York: HarperBusiness, 1993.

Ebener, Dan R. *Blessings for Leaders: Leadership Wisdom from the Beatitudes.* Collegeville, MN: Liturgical Press, 2012.

———. "On Becoming a Servant Leader." *Sojourners*, February 2011.

———. *Pastoral Leadership: Best Practices for Church Leaders.* Mahwah, NJ: Paulist Press, 2018.

———. *Servant Leadership Models for Your Parish.* Mahwah, NJ: Paulist Press, 2010.

Ebener, Dan R., and Frederick L. Smith. *Strategic Planning: An Interactive Process for Leaders.* Mahwah, NJ: Paulist Press, 2015.

Edersheim, Elizabeth Haas, and Peter F. Drucker. *The Definitive Drucker.* New York: McGraw-Hill, 2007.

Edinger, Scott K., and Laurie Sain. *The Hidden Leader: Discover and Develop Greatness within Your Company.* New York: AMACOM, 2015.

Eichholz, Juan Carlos. *Adaptive Capacity: How Organizations Can Thrive in a Changing World.* Greenwich, CT: LID Publishing, 2014.

Fisher, Roger, and Scott Brown. *Getting Together: Building Relationships as We Negotiate.* New York: Penguin, 1989.

Fisher, Roger, William Ury, and Bruce Patton. *Getting to Yes: Negotiating an Agreement without Giving In.* 2nd ed. London: Random House Business Books, 1999.

Follett, Mary Parker. *Freedom and Co-ordination: Lectures in Business Organization.* London: Routledge, 2015.

Frankl, Viktor Emil. *Man's Search for Meaning.* Mini book ed. Boston: Beacon Press, 2006.

French, John, and Bertram Raven. "The Bases of Social Power." In *Studies in Social Power*, edited by Dorwin Cartwright, 150–57. Ann Arbor: Research Center for Group Dynamics, Institute for Social Research, University of Michigan, 1959.

Friedland, Daniel. *Leading Well from Within: A Neuroscience and Mindfulness-Based Framework for Conscious Leadership.* San Diego: SuperSmartHealth, 2016.

Gillihan, Seth. *Retrain Your Brain: Cognitive Behavioral Therapy in 7 Weeks.* Berkeley: Althea Press, 2016.

Glasl, Friedrich. *Konfliktmanagement: ein Handbuch für Führungskräfte, Beraterinnen und Berater.* Aktualisierte Auflage. Bern: Haupt Verlag, 2013.

Goleman, Daniel. *Emotional Intelligence.* 10th anniversary ed. New York: Bantam Books, 2005.

Goulston, Mark. *Just Listen: Discover the Secret to Getting through to Absolutely Anyone.* New York: American Management Association, 2010.

Graen, G., and J. Cashman. "A Role Making Model of Leadership in Formal Organizations: A Developmental Approach." In *Leadership Frontiers*, edited by J. G. Hunt and L. L. Larson, 143–65. Kent, OH: Kent State University Press, 1975.

Graen, George B., and Mary Uhl-Bien. "Relationship-Based Approach to Leadership: Development of Leader-Member Exchange (LMX) Theory of Leadership over 25 Years; Applying a Multi-level Multi-domain Perspective." *Leadership Quarterly* 6, no. 2 (1995): 219–47.

Greenleaf, Robert K. *Servant Leadership: A Journey into the Nature of Legitimate Power and Greatness*. Mahwah, NJ: Paulist Press, 1977.

Greenleaf, Robert K., Hamilton Beazley, Julie Beggs, and Larry C. Spears. *The Servant-Leader Within: A Transformative Path*. Mahwah, NJ: Paulist Press, 2003.

Heifetz, Ronald A. *Leadership without Easy Answers*. Cambridge, MA: Belknap Press of Harvard University Press, 1994.

Heifetz, Ronald A., Alexander Grashow, and Martin Linsky. *The Practice of Adaptive Leadership: Tools and Tactics for Changing Your Organization and the World*. Boston: Harvard Business Press, 2009.

Heifetz, Ronald A., and Donald L. Laurie. "The Work of Leadership." *Harvard Business Review*, February 1997.

Heifetz, Ronald A., and Martin Linsky. *Leadership on the Line: Staying Alive through the Dangers of Leading*. Boston: Harvard Business School Press, 2002.

———. "A Survival Guide for Leaders." *Harvard Business Review*, June 2002.

Hersey, Paul, and Ken Blanchard. "Life Cycle Theory of Leadership." *Training and Development Journal* 23 (1969): 26–34.

Herzberg, Frederic. "The Motivation-Hygiene Concept and Problems of Manpower." *Personnel Administration* 27, no. 1 (1964): 3–7.

———. *One More Time: How Do You Motivate Employees*. Boston: Harvard Business Review, 1968.

Hofstede, Geert H. *Culture's Consequences: International Differences in Work-Related Values*. Abridged ed. Cross-Cultural Research and Methodology Series. Beverly Hills: SAGE Publications, 1984.

House, Robert J. *A 1976 Theory of Charismatic Leadership. Working Paper Series 76-06*. Toronto: Faculty of Management Studies, University of Toronto, 1977.

———. "A Path Goal Theory of Leader Effectiveness." *Administrative Science Quarterly* 16, no. 3 (September 1971): 321. https://doi.org/10.2307/2391905.

———. "Path-Goal Theory of Leadership: Lessons, Legacy, and a Reformulated Theory." *The Leadership Quarterly* 7, no. 3 (September 1996): 323–52. https://doi.org/10.1016/S1048-9843(96)90024-7.

House, Robert J., and Terrence R. Mitchell. "Path-Goal Theory of Leadership." *Contemporary Business* 3 (1974): 81–98.

Isaacs, William. *Dialogue and the Art of Thinking Together: A Pioneering Approach to Communicating in Business and in Life*. New York: Currency, 1999.

Janis, Irving L. "Groupthink." *Psychology Today* 5, no. 6 (1971): 43–46, 74–76.

Jehn, K. A., and E. A. Mannix. "The Dynamic Nature of Conflict: A Longitudinal Study of Intragroup Conflict and Group Performance." *Academy of Management Journal* 44, no. 2 (April 1, 2001): 238–51.

Jehn, Karen A. "A Multimethod Examination of the Benefits and Detriments of Intragroup Conflict." *Administrative Science Quarterly* 40, no. 2 (June 1995): 256. https://doi.org/10.2307/2393638.

Johnson, Robert, and Adam Cureton. "Kant's Moral Philosophy." In *The Stanford Encyclopedia of Philosophy*, edited by Edward N. Zalta. Stanford, CA: Stanford University Metaphysics Research Lab, 2019. https://plato.stanford.edu/archives/spr2019/entries/kant-moral/.

Judge, Timothy A., Joyce E. Bono, Remus Ilies, and Megan W. Gerhardt. "Personality and Leadership: A Qualitative and Quantitative Review." *Journal of Applied Psychology* 87, no. 4 (2002): 765–80. https://doi.org/10.1037/0021-9010.87.4.765.

Judge, Timothy A., Amy E. Colbert, and Remus Ilies. "Intelligence and Leadership: A Quantitative Review and Test of Theoretical Propositions." *Journal of Applied Psychology* 89, no. 3 (2004): 542–52. https://doi.org/10.1037/0021-9010.89.3.542.

Judge, Timothy A., Ronald F. Piccolo, and Remus Ilies. "The Forgotten Ones? The Validity of Consideration and Initiating Structure in Leadership Research." *Journal of Applied Psychology* 89, no. 1 (2004): 36–51. https://doi.org/10.1037/0021-9010.89.1.36.

Katz, Robert L. "Skills of an Effective Administrator." *Harvard Business Review*, 1974.

Keeley, Michael. "The Trouble with Transformational Leadership: Toward a Federalist Ethic for Organizations." *Business Ethics Quarterly* 5, no. 1 (January 1995): 67–96. https://doi.org/10.2307/3857273.

Kellerman, Barbara. *Followership: How Followers Are Creating Change and Changing Leaders*. Leadership for the Common Good. Boston: Harvard Business School Press, 2008.

Kennedy, Edward M. "Eulogy for Robert Kennedy." *New York Times*, June 9, 1968.

Kirkpatrick, Shelley A., and Edwin A. Locke. "Leadership: Do Traits Matter?" *The Executive* 5, no. 2 (1991): 48–60.

Knights, David, and Majella O'Leary. "Leadership, Ethics and Responsibility to the Other." *Journal of Business Ethics* 67, no. 2 (2006): 125–37.

Kotter, John P. *Leading Change*. Boston: Harvard Business School Press, 1996.

———. *A Sense of Urgency*. Boston: Harvard Business Press, 2008.

———. "What Leaders Really Do." *Harvard Business Review*, 1990.

Kouzes, James M., and Barry Z. Posner. *The Leadership Challenge: How to Make Extraordinary Things Happen in Organizations*. 6th ed. Hoboken, NJ: Leadership Challenge, A Wiley Brand, 2017.

———. *The Truth about Leadership: The No-Fads, Heart-of-the-Matter Facts You Need to Know*. San Francisco: Jossey-Bass, 2010.

Lama, Dalai. *How to Practice: The Way to a Meaningful Life*. Translated by Jeffrey Hopkins. New York: Atria Books, 2003.

Lefton, Robert Eugene, and V. Ralph Buzzotta. *Leadership through People Skills*. New York: McGraw-Hill, 2004.

Lencioni, Patrick. *The Five Dysfunctions of a Team: A Leadership Fable*. San Francisco: Jossey-Bass, 2002.

MacGregor, Douglas. *The Human Side of Enterprise*. New York: McGraw-Hill, 1960.

Manz, Charles C., and Henry P. Sims. *Business without Bosses: How Self-Managing Teams Are Building High-Performing Companies*. New York: Wiley, 1995.

Marquardt, Michael J. *Leading with Questions: How Leaders Find the Right Solutions by Knowing What to Ask*. Revised and updated ed. San Francisco: Jossey-Bass, 2014.

Marturano, Janice. *Finding the Space to Lead: A Practical Guide to Mindful Leadership*. London: Bloomsbury, 2015.

Maslow, A. H. "A Theory of Human Motivation." *Psychological Review* 50, no. 4 (July 1943): 370–96. https://doi.org/10.1037/h0054346.

Maslow, Abraham H. *The Farther Reaches of Human Nature*. New York: Arkana, 1993.

———. *Maslow on Management*. New York: John Wiley, 1998.

McKinsey Report. "Soft Skills for a Hard World." (blog), 2020. https://www.mckinsey.com/business-functions/transformation/our-insights/five-fifty-the-changeable-organization.

Megginson, Leon C. "Lessons from Europe for American Business." *The Southwestern Social Science Quarterly* 44, no. 1 (June 1963): 3–13.

Moss Kanter, Rosabeth. "What Inexperienced Leaders Get Wrong (Hint: Management)." *Harvard Business Review*, November 21, 2013.

Nadler, David A., and Michael L. Tushman. "Beyond the Charismatic Leader: Leadership and Organizational Change." *California Management Review* 32, no. 2 (January 1990): 77–97. https://doi.org/10.2307/41166606.

Nahavandi, Afsaneh. *The Art and Science of Leadership*. 4th ed. Upper Saddle River, NJ: Pearson/Prentice Hall, 2006.

———. *The Art and Science of Leadership*. 7th ed. Boston: Pearson, 2015.

Nanus, Burt. *Leading the Way to Organization Renewal*. Management Master Series. Portland, OR: Productivity Press, 1996.

Northouse, Peter Guy. *Leadership: Theory and Practice*. 6th ed. Thousand Oaks, CA: SAGE, 2013.

Organ, Dennis W. *Organizational Citizenship Behavior: The Good Soldier Syndrome*. Issues in Organization and Management Series. Lexington, MA: Lexington Books, 1988.

Organ, Dennis W., Philip M. Podsakoff, and Scott Bradley MacKenzie. *Organizational Citizenship Behavior: Its Nature, Antecedents, and Consequences*. Foundations for Organizational Science. Thousand Oaks, CA: SAGE Publications, 2006.

Pearce, Joseph Chilton. *The Biology of Transcendence: A Blueprint of the Human Spirit*. Rochester, VT: Park Street Press, 2004.

Pink, Daniel H. *Drive: The Surprising Truth about What Motivates Us*. First paperback ed. New York: Riverhead Books, 2011.

Post, Jerrold M. "Narcissism and the Charismatic Leader-Follower Relationship." *Political Psychology* 7, no. 4 (December 1986): 675–87. https://doi.org/10.2307/3791208.

Price, Terry L. *Leadership Ethics: An Introduction.* Cambridge: Cambridge University Press, 2008.

Richards, Randy L. *Conflict and Collaboration: The Search for the Integrative Space.* Rock Island, IL: Richards, 2017.

Rock, David. *Your Brain at Work: Strategies for Overcoming Distraction, Regaining Focus, and Working Smarter All Day Long.* New York: Harper Business, 2009.

Rost, Joseph C. *Leadership for the Twenty-First Century.* New York: Praeger, 1991.

Rubin, Robert S., Erich C. Dierdorff, and Michael E. Brown. "Do Ethical Leaders Get Ahead? Exploring Ethical Leadership and Promotability." *Business Ethics Quarterly* 20, no. 02 (April 2010): 215–36. https://doi.org/10.5840/beq201020216.

Ryan, Richard M., and Edward L. Deci. "Overview of Self-Determination Theory: An Organismic-Dialectical Perspective." In *Handbook of Self-Determination Research,* edited by E. L. Deci and R. M. Ryan, 3–33. Rochester, NY: University of Rochester Press, 2002.

———. "Self-Regulation and the Problem of Human Autonomy: Does Psychology Need Choice, Self-Determination, and Will?" *Journal of Personality* 74, no. 6 (December 2006): 1557–86. https://doi.org/10.1111/j.1467-6494.2006.00420.x.

Ryan, Richard M., Julius Kuhl, and Edward L. Deci. "Nature and Autonomy: An Organizational View of Social and Neurobiological Aspects of Self-Regulation in Behavior and Development." *Development and Psychopathology* 9, no. 4 (December 1997): 701–28. https://doi.org/10.1017/S0954579497001405.

Sashkin, Marshall, and Molly G. Sashkin. *Leadership That Matters: The Critical Factors for Making a Difference in People's Lives and Organizations' Success.* San Francisco: Berrett-Koehler, 2003.

Scharmer, Claus Otto, and Katrin Kaufer. *Leading from the Emerging Future: From Ego-System to Eco-System Economies.* San Francisco: Berrett-Koehler Publishers, 2013.

Schein, Edgar H. *Humble Consulting: How to Provide Real Help Faster.* Oakland, CA: Berrett-Koehler Publishers, 2016.

———. *Humble Inquiry: The Gentle Art of Asking Instead of Telling.* San Francisco: Berrett-Koehler Publishers, 2013.

Sinek, Simon. *Start with Why: How Great Leaders Inspire Everyone to Take Action.* New York, NY: Portfolio, Penguin, 2011.

Stogdill, Ralph M. "Personal Factors Associated with Leadership: A Survey of the Literature." *The Journal of Psychology* 25, no. 1 (January 1948): 35–71. https://doi.org/10.1080/00223980.1948.9917362.

Thomas, Kenneth W. "Conflict and Negotiation Processes in Organizations." In *Handbook of Industrial and Organizational Psychology,* edited by M. D. Dunnette and L. M. Hough, 651–717. Palo Alto, CA: Consulting Psychologists Press, 1992.

———. *Intrinsic Motivation at Work: Building Energy and Commitment*. San Francisco: Berrett-Koehler, 2002.

Ventura, Michael P. *Applied Empathy: The New Language of Leadership*. New York: Touchstone, 2018.

Weber, Max, and Talcott Parsons. *The Theory of Social and Economic Organization*. Translated by T. Parsons and A. M. Henderson. New York: Free Press, 1997.

Wheatley, Margaret. "Some Friends and I Started Talking." *DailyGood: News That Inspires* (blog), January 7, 2014. http://www.dailygood.org/story/614/some-friends-and-i-started-talking/.

White, Ralph K., and Ronald Lippitt. *Autocracy and Democracy: An Experimental Inquiry*. Westport, CT: Greenwood Press, 1972.

Wooden, John, and Steve Jamison. *Wooden on Leadership*. New York: McGraw-Hill, 2005.

INDEX

You can contact the authors at the following email addresses:
Dan at EbenerDanR@sau.edu, and Borna at BJalsen@zsem.hr.